Happy Christmas
'92

Tom Ferris

IRISH RAILWAYS

IN COLOUR

From Steam to Diesel
1955 - 1967

Gill and Macmillan

To Michael
for encouraging my obsession
and to Elizabeth
who has had to put up with it.

First Published by
Midland Publishing Limited
in 1992.

Published in Ireland by
Gill and Macmillan Limited
Goldenbridge
Dublin 8
with associated companies in
Auckland, Budapest, Gaborone, Harare,
Hong Kong, Kampala, Kuala Lumpur,
Lagos, London, Madras, Manzini,
Melbourne, Mexico City, Nairobi,
New York, Singapore, Sydney,
Tokyo, Windhoek.

0 7171 1989 0

Printed in Hong Kong

A catalogue record is available for this
book from the British Library.

Designed by
Midland Publishing
and Stephen Thompson Associates

Text typeset
in 8 on 10 and 9 on 11pt Garamond
and Gill Sans

CONTENTS

Front cover:
Top: **WT class No.4 leaves Belfast
on a Sunday School Special in July 1966.**
Derek Young.
Bottom: **Panorama of Dublin's
North Wall freight yards in 1956.**
John Edgington.

Frontispiece:
**CDR class 5 2-6-4T No.4 *Meenglas*
pauses at Castlefinn on 22nd June 1959,
her mixed train topped by the ex-B&L
coach and tailed by one of the CDR brake
vans in the red and cream livery.**
Michael Costeloe.

Back cover:
Top: **Railbus 2A at Manorhamilton.**
Gerry Douglas.
Bottom: **One of the original C&L 4-4-0Ts
about to depart for Arigna.**
Harry Luff.

PREFACE

The period from 1955-1967 was a momentous one for the Irish railway network. It saw the virtual elimination of the steam locomotive, the end of the narrow gauge and even a threat to the very existence of railways within Northern Ireland. For those fortunate enough to observe Ireland's railways in this period it was a time of considerable interest. New diesel locomotives and railcars shared the tracks with steam engines, some built as long ago as the 1860s, whilst others were less than ten years old.

This book is an attempt to convey a flavour of these years using the medium of colour photographs. We are most fortunate that a few photographers saw the need to record Ireland's railways in colour despite the difficulties imposed by film as slow as ASA8 or ASA10, and the high cost of colour film at the time. In the mid 1950s a roll of 36 exposure colour film could cost nearly £2, a not inconsiderable sum in those days.

Inevitably there are gaps in the record. Some classes of locomotives and stretches of line which I would very much like to have included are absent simply because I have been unable to find them recorded in colour. To some extent, availability of material has determined the shape of the book, but as the picture research progressed, I was more enthused by what the photographers had recorded in colour than saddened by what they had missed.

Some pictures included may not be of the highest quality in technical terms. Certain types of colour film have a tendency to fade with age or are susceptible to reticulation and other forms of deterioration. In some cases I have given priority to historical interest over technical perfection and I hope readers will be understanding of this necessity.

What follows makes no claim to being a comprehensive or detailed survey of Irish railways in this period. In the space available it is only possible to convey a series of impressions, but at least it will be possible to remind ourselves just how beautiful the blue engines and teak coaches of the Great Northern Railway were, the shade of red used on the County Donegal and how the Irish weather quickly subverted the shiny silver/aluminium finish of Coras Iompair Eireann's first mainline diesels.

ACKNOWLEDGMENTS

I came to do this book almost by accident. As a railway enthusiast I was surprised that so little was in print in book form about the railways of my native land and as a publisher I was aware that it might be commercially viable to do for the first time a colour album on Irish railways. It was only when one or two prospective authors, much better qualified to do the book than myself, were unable to get involved with the project because of other commitments that, rather than let a good idea slip, I decided to do it myself.

A great many people have helped me in the course of putting the book together. It is fair to say that it could not have been done without the assistance of my good friend Clifton Flewitt who put me in touch with most of the photographers whose work is represented in the book. Another long standing friend Des McGlynn was particularly helpful with his constructive criticism along the way and for his contributions on the subject of the early CIE diesels on which I was not terribly well informed. My colleague at Midland Publishing, Chris Salter must be thanked for piloting the book through the conception and production stages, a task made more difficult for him by having the author hovering over his shoulder a lot of the time like an expectant father.

Above all else this book is a tribute to the photographers whose work it features. Their foresight in recording the Irish Railway network in the 1950s and '60s in colour was commendable. At a time when colour film was slow and expensive and when they were a lot younger and on limited budgets, they did a fine job in capturing the actuality of those years for future generations. The photographers whose work is featured in this book are; A.L.Barnett, Greg Child, Michael Costeloe, J.J.Davis, the late Gerry Douglas whose collection is now in the care of Chris Banks, who has kindly given me access to the Irish material, John Edgington, Charles Friel, Harry Luff, Des McGlynn, F.W.Shuttleworth, Richard Whitford and Derek Young. It would be difficult to exaggerate the assistance and hospitality which the main contributors have given me in the course of my research.

The railway company crests used in this book are on display at the Cyril Fry Model Railway at Malahide Castle in Dublin and are reproduced here with the kind permission of Dublin Tourism.

A final word of thanks to my wife Elizabeth for putting up so cheerfully with the formation of Midland Publishing Limited, the writing of this book and a thousand other things in the course of her third pregnancy and to the existing 'baby ferrets' for keeping out of my study and not touching the slides. The usual and necessary author's caveats about all the aforenamed persons being absolved from responsibility for the finished product go without saying.

Tom Ferris
Shrewsbury, January 1992

RAILWAYS IN IRELAND
IN 1957

STANDARD BROAD GAUGE
NARROW GAUGE

At its zenith in 1920 the route mileage of the Irish railway system stood at 3,442 (this figure includes both broad and narrow gauge lines). By the beginning of the period covered in this book, 1955, it had fallen to 2,727 miles which was still a respectable figure given the size of the island and its relatively small population.

From 1957 onwards the system began to contract rapidly until it had stabilised in the 1970s at around 1,450 route miles. The most savage cutbacks occurred in Northern Ireland where by the end of 1965 all of the former Great Northern Railway system except the main Dublin-Belfast line and the branch from Lisburn to Antrim had been closed. The only other lines surviving in the province were those serving Bangor, Larne, Portrush and Londonderry via Coleraine. The Irish narrow gauge lines had been in progressive decline since the 1920s when there were 537 miles of 3ft gauge track. By 1955 no narrow gauge lines survived in Northern Ireland, but 190 miles of the 3ft gauge continued to be operated in the Irish Republic though all of this had gone by 1961.

In 1955 there were five distinct railway operators in Ireland, the Ulster Transport Authority, the Great Northern Railway Board, Coras Iompair Eireann, the County Donegal Railways Joint Committee and the Sligo, Leitrim and Northern Counties Railway. The UTA was set up by the Northern Ireland legislature in 1948 to take over railway and road transport undertakings located wholly within the province. The railways involved were the Belfast & County Down Railway and the lines of the old Belfast & Northern Counties Railway which since 1923 had been run by the Northern Counties Committee of its British parent, the London Midland and Scottish Railway. The initials UTA are usually hissed through clenched teeth by railway enthusiasts. The Authority and its political masters were overtly anti-railway. It quickly closed down most of the branch lines of the NCC system and all of the B&CDR with the exception of the Bangor line. The pogrom continued with the closure of all the cross border lines of the GNR in 1957 and the GNR's

'Derry Road' along with the Newry and Warrenpoint branch in 1965. It is a paradox that despite the wholesale line closures, steam traction was not finally eliminated from the UTA and its much more enlightened successor Northern Ireland Railways until 1970 when the survivors of the WT class tank locomotives, the last main line steam engines in regular use in the British Isles, were withdrawn.

The Great Northern Railway Board was set up in 1953 in an act of cross border co-operation unusual for those times. By the early 1950s, despite the efforts of a progressive and enterprising management, the GNR was in a parlous financial condition. The governments of Northern Ireland and the Republic bought the railway for £4.5 million and set up the Board to run it. Five members were appointed by each government and this state of affairs continued until 1958 when the Board was dissolved and its assets were divided between the UTA and CIE. Happily for those interested in railways the Board continued the ethos of the old company and blue engines and teak finished coaches were still the order of the day.

All the railways wholly located in the Irish Republic were operated by CIE. (The English translation of Coras Iompair Eireann is, the Irish Transport Company). CIE was set up by the Irish government in 1945, initially as a private company, though with financial support from the public purse. It was fully nationalised in 1950. The company was responsible for road, rail and canal services in the Republic. The parallels between the ownership and operation of the railways in Britain and Ireland are striking. The privately owned Irish railways were forced to amalgamate by government in 1925 to form the Great Southern Railway, the grouping of railways in Britain into four large companies occurred in 1923. In Ireland nationalisation came two years after it had occurred in Britain.

The GSR had made little effort to modernise its system. Very few new locomotives and carriages were built in its 20 year existence. In 1948 CIE commissioned Sir James Milne, the last

General Manager of the British Great Western Railway, to report on the state of its railways. Milne must have been surprised to say the least by what he found. To give but one telling statistic, the average age of the locomotives in the CIE fleet was fifty-one years. Milne did not believe that the level of traffic on Ireland's railways justified the heavy capital expenditure which a programme of dieselisation called for. He even advocated that new steam locomotives should be constructed at Inchicore. However no Irish equivalent of British Railways' standard locos were ever built. Instead the Board of CIE decided to embark on a rapid programme of dieselisation. In 1951 the first of a fleet of sixty AEC-engined diesel railcars, similar to those already in service with the GNR, were delivered. This was followed in 1953 by the issuing of tenders for over 100 diesel locomotives. The first of the A Class main line diesels were delivered from Metropolitan-Vickers in 1955; other locomotives for secondary and branch line duties quickly followed. Commendable as such bold investment in the railway system was, no prototypes had been ordered and tested, the infrastructure to maintain such sophisticated machines had to be rapidly developed from scratch and the CIE diesel locomotive fleet had its fair share of problems as might have been expected with machines ordered straight off the drawing board.

One predictable effect of the arrival of the diesels was that rapid inroads were made into the steam fleet. Though some steam locomotives remained active into the early 1960s on the CIE system, by 1959 it was rare for a steam engine to be used on regular passenger services in the Irish Republic.

Four Irish narrow gauge systems survived into the period covered by this book. One, that of Bord na Mona (the Turf Board), was purely industrial and is still going strong. Of the other three, the West and South Clare lines and the Cavan & Leitrim were under the control of CIE, and the County Donegal system retained its independent identity to the end. The rest of the once extensive network of 3ft gauge lines had been closed by 1955.

The contrast between the two CIE controlled narrow gauge lines could not have been more marked. The Clare lines had been completely dieselised by 1955. Passenger services were operated by railcars and three specially built diesel locomotives handled the freight. Despite the modernisation of its rolling stock the Clare lines were closed in 1961, though they had the distinction of being the last remnants of the 3ft gauge to remain open for traffic. The C&L, on the other hand, far from being modernised remained a sublime anachronism. Steam operated to the end; it had acquired over the years rolling stock from other narrow gauge lines as they had succumbed. Locomotives or other stock from the Cork, Blackrock & Passage Railway (closed 1932), the Tralee & Dingle (closed 1953), and the Clogher Valley Railway (closed 1941), could be seen in action on the C&L up to its own demise.

The final narrow gauge system operating in our period was the County Donegal Railway, or to give its full title, the County Donegal Railways Joint Committee. The CDR was the only sizeable joint line in Ireland. This had come about through the acquisition of various narrow gauge lines in County Donegal by the GNR and the English Midland Railway in 1906. The CDR was a well managed railway which pioneered the use of diesel railcars for passenger services from the 1920s onwards. Steam traction was retained for freight and excursion traffic. The distinctive CDR livery of geranium red for locomotives and red and cream for railcars and carriages was a delight to behold and there was considerable sadness both among railway enthusiasts and for those who lived in the area served by the CDR when the last trains ran on the 31st December 1959.

The final railway operator in Ireland was the last truly independent standard gauge railway company in the British Isles, the Sligo, Leitrim & Northern Counties Railway. Because it straddled the border it escaped absorption into the GSR in 1925 and by dint of its parlous

financial condition, no other company was interested in acquiring it. Running from Enniskillen in Northern Ireland to Sligo in the Republic, the SL&NCR owed its existence to that staple of Ireland's economy, cattle. Passenger services were operated in the main by a railcar and a railbus, freight by a small stud of 0-6-4 tanks, identified not by numbers which they never possessed, but by names.

These included the last two conventional steam locomotives built for an Irish railway which were delivered in 1951. They were supplied by the manufacturers Beyer Peacock on a sort of hire-purchase agreement. The impecunious SL&NCR was never able to afford to buy the locos, which as a consequence carried small plates on their bunkers, indicating that they were the property of their makers and not their operators. It is ironic that despite its hand to mouth existence for so many years the closure of the SL&NCR finally came about because of the Northern Ireland government's decision to close the GNR lines to Enniskillen in 1957 which deprived the SL&NCR of an outlet for the cattle which comprised so much of its business.

Our travels in Ireland will be concluded with a look at the railway owned tramways and some industrial railway systems. The tramways were both operated by the GNR, the fabled Fintona horse tram and the equally famous Hill of Howth tramway. Ireland has never been heavily industrialised and has little in the way of coal or mineral resources therefore industrial railway systems were not common. It is appropriate that two of the best known systems were concerned with the production of those distinctly Irish products, turf and stout.

The great charm of the railways of Ireland in the 1950s and the early 1960s was the contrast between the new and the old. In the Republic one could see brand new diesels hauling ancient bogie and even six wheeled carriages. As new coaches were built they were often introduced in a seemingly random manner adding further interest to the

make up of the trains. Venerable steam locomotives, notably the J15 class, built by the Great Southern & Western Railway from 1866 to 1903, could be observed hauling or shunting the latest stock. Freight trains were invariably composed of loose coupled four wheeled vehicles and a great variety of different wagons could be seen both on goods trains and on sidings around the system.

In the north the NCC section of the UTA had an excellent fleet of modern steam locomotives. These contrasted with both the early NCC railcars and the new types being introduced by the UTA. The uncluttered lines and sheer elegance of ex-GNR steam locomotives could still be appreciated up to the mid-60s in Northern Ireland, and the particular charm of the Irish narrow gauge is still fondly remembered to this day.

I hope that in the following pages the reader will discover for the first time or rediscover the delights that the railways of Ireland had to offer at this time. We will travel from north to south on the 5ft 3in gauge and in the opposite direction on the narrow gauge. We will see steam, diesel, electric and of course horse traction on our travels. I hope the journey will be a pleasant one for you and if it imparts half the pleasure that I have had in compiling it then I think you will have enjoyed it.

Chapter One

THE ULSTER

TRANSPORT AUTHORITY

The UTA came into being in 1948 through legislation enacted by the Northern Ireland Parliament. Its brief was to take over road and rail transport undertakings in the province. The railways involved were the B&CDR and the NCC.

Most of the B&CDR system was closed in January 1950. Its steam locos had all been withdrawn by 1953 though one, a 4-4-2T No.30 built in 1901, was preserved by the UTA and is now in Belfast Transport Museum. The remaining part of the B&CDR, the Bangor line, had the distinction of being the first line in the British Isles to be completely dieselised, in 1954. The new Multiple Engined Diesels (MEDs) began to arrive in 1951 and provided a far superior service for Bangor commuters than the old six-wheelers of which B&CDR trains were often comprised. One B&CDR locomotive remained active into the 1960s. This was No.28 an eight wheel diesel with electric transmission built in 1937 by the Belfast shipbuilders Harland & Wolff. The Bangor line did see steam locomotives from time to time in the years after dieselisation. Excursions were run to Bangor from many parts of Northern Ireland, often organised by Sunday Schools. These brought steam back to the 'County Down' as did permanent way and works trains. All these workings came to an end in 1965 when the Belfast Central Railway was closed. This line connected the former B&CDR and GNR systems and its closure cut the Bangor line off from the

rest of the Irish railway network. In the 1970s this link was reinstated by NIR and Bangor line trains were diverted to the new Belfast Central station, the old B&CDR terminus at Queen's Quay being closed to passengers.

The LMS had supplied its Ulster offshoot with a fine stud of modern steam locos which the UTA inherited in 1948. Between 1933 and 1942 fifteen of the W Class 2-6-0 Moguls were built. The influence of the Derby works of the LMS could be clearly be seen in the appearance and design of these locos. They were followed by the WT Class of 2-6-4 Tank engines, universally known as the Jeeps, introduced from 1946-50. These machines bore many similarities to the LMS 2-6-4T designs of Stanier and Fairburn and were used on all sorts of duties, not just on the ex-NCC lines, but on the ex-GNR lines following the demise of the GNR Board in 1958. The arrival of the Moguls and Jeeps allowed many of the older engines to be scrapped, however some of the 'Castle' Class 4-4-0s and the V Class 0-6-0s survived into our period.

The NCC was early in the field with diesel railcars. The first of these was introduced in 1933. It was powered by Leyland petrol engines and could be driven from either end. This was followed by three bizarre creations which had elevated lookouts for the driver. The idea of this was that, if the railcar was marshalled in the middle of a train, or if it was pushing a trailer, the driver from his elevated fastness, could

see the line ahead. In fact the driver's view was very restricted by this arrangement. During the war an altercation on the Portrush branch between a railcar and a cow put an end to this rather dubious operating practice.

Despite the modernity of the steam locos on the NCC section of the UTA, it was inevitable that with the success of the diesels on the Bangor line, the UTA would provide diesels for the rest of its lines. From 1957 onwards a new class of railcar was built by the UTA. Called the Multi-Purpose Diesel (MPD), they were built on the frames of former locomotive hauled carriages and were multi-purpose to the extent that they were even able to haul freight trains. Their arrival signalled the end for steam on trains to Portrush and Londonderry, though as we shall see some of the Moguls found further employment on the ex-GNR lines to Derry and Dublin.

The Jeeps soldiered on and in the late 1960s were used on the famous spoil trains conveying stone from a quarry at Magheramorne near Larne, which was used to build the M2 motorway along the shores of Belfast Lough near the former NCC terminus at York Road. Though slightly outside our period and operated by the UTA's successor Northern Ireland Railways, the spoil trains and their grimy Jeeps merit inclusion in this chapter as these were the last regular steam workings, not just in Ireland but in the whole of the British Isles.

THE BANGOR LINE DIESELS

The only part of the B&CDR to escape closure in 1950 was the busy commuter line from Belfast to Bangor. Following the success of a three car prototype diesel train introduced in 1951, the UTA decided to dieselise the Bangor line as soon as possible. The new trains known as Multiple Engined Diesels (MEDs) could run in three or six car formations. They were equipped with sliding recessed doors under the control of the guards, of a type normally seen only on tube trains at this time.

The MEDs allowed the Bangor line to become the first in the British Isles to have a fully dieselised regular passenger service.

Top: **Two MED units headed by car No.14 are seen leaving Bangor station on 7th April 1961, forming the 6.10pm service to Belfast Queen's Quay.**
Richard Whitford.

Lower: **Bangor line MEDs did not often venture off their native heath. However on 26th June 1961 a six car formation was recorded at Adelaide having worked a football special to the nearby Windsor Park.** Richard Whitford.

THE LAST B&CDR LOCOMOTIVE

Though the B&CDR steam fleet had been scrapped by 1956, one B&CDR locomotive survived in service until the late 1960s. This was No.28, an eight wheeled diesel electric machine produced by the Belfast shipbuilding firm of Harland & Wolff in 1937. The usual B&CDR practice in allocating numbers to locomotives was to give the newcomer the number of the one it had replaced in the fleet. Thus was the new diesel electric treated, taking the number of a recently scrapped 2-4-2T. The locomotive spent most of its later career shunting at the ex-GNR terminus of Great Victoria Street in Belfast.

Below: **No.28 is seen at the former GNR goods depot at Grosvenor Road in Belfast on 13th March 1967. The distinctive H&W builder's plate can be seen just below the roof in the centre of the cab.** Richard Whitford.

Above: **On 19th July 1963 No. 28 was shunting goods wagons outside Great Victoria Street station.** Richard Whitford.

11

STEAM ON THE 'COUNTY DOWN'

Though scheduled steam services ceased in 1954, seaside excursion traffic continued to bring steam locomotives to Bangor up to 1965. Because of weight restrictions on the bridge which joined the 'County Down' to the rest of the network the lighter ex-GNR classes were favoured for these trains.

Top: **Class UG No.49 (GNR No.149) arriving at Bangor on Easter Monday, 3rd April 1961, with an excursion from Strabane. The locomotive is in UTA lined black but most of the coaches retain their GNR livery.** Richard Whitford.

Lower: **U class 4-4-0 No.68 (GNR No.205) appropriately named** *Down* **gets under way with a return seven coach excursion train to Portadown. Though nearly three years had elapsed since the demise of the GNRB, the loco and its train retain their GNR livery.** Richard Whitford.

Opposite: **On 19th June 1965 UG class 0-6-0 No.48 (GNR No.146) heads an excursion to Bangor past the closed Kinnegar Halt between Belfast and Holywood. Just visible on the runway at Sydenham is a Short** *Belfast* **freighter aircraft.** Richard Whitford.

Left: **Some of the last steam workings on the Bangor line, before the closure of the Belfast Central Railway in 1965 cut the line off from the rest of the Irish railway network, were in connection with the construction of a new halt at Crawfordsburn. On 12th August 1965 UG class No.48 (GNR No.146) is climbing through Marino with a ballast train in support of this work.** Derek Young.

Right: **Permanent way and other works trains also brought steam to the Bangor Line. The former GNR weedkiller train is seen near Tillysburn between Belfast and Hollywood on 7th June 1965. The gentleman standing on the wagon in the middle of the train is dispensing weedkiller. The train is hauled by UG class No.48 (GNR No.146).** Derek Young.

Below: **Having traversed the former Belfast Central Railway, UG class No.48 (GNR No.146) brings its sleeper train down to join the Bangor line at Ballymacarrett Junction on 12th August 1965. The remains of the B&CDR loco shed at Queen's Quay can be seen in the background.** Derek Young.

THE NCC MOGULS

The W class 2-6-0s, fifteen in number, built between 1933 and 1942 revolutionised services on the NCC. The first four were constructed at Derby; the rest assembled in Belfast with parts supplied from England. The broad outlines of the design were worked out in Belfast under the supervsion of H. P. Stewart, the NCC locomotive engineer, but the completed engines owed much to LMS practice. The new engines had the standard 6ft driving wheels used on the existing NCC 4-4-0s. They weighed 62½ tons, had a tractive effort of 22,160 lbs and worked at a boiler pressure of 200 pounds per square inch. All but two of the class, Nos 102 and 104, were named and were at first turned out in LMS/NCC red. One engine was named after King Edward VIII and unlike other British locos which took his name, No.98 retained the name after the King's abdication. The W class were displaced from their own main line with the arrival of new UTA diesel railcars in the late 1950s. However members of the class found plenty of work on the former GNR lines to Dublin and Derry and the last survivors were not withdrawn until 1965.

Right: **1942 built Mogul No.104, one of the two which were never named, storms out of Belfast Great Victoria Street station on 23rd May 1963 with the 9.20 am train to Dublin.** Greg Child

Below: **A fine portrait of No.97** *Earl of Ulster* **at Portrush in 1956; the fireman is bailing out the fire in preparation for the return trip to Belfast. Note the typical B&NCR somersault signal in the background and the tablet catching equipment on the cabside.**
Gerry Douglas /courtesy Chris Banks.

Mogul No. 98 *King Edward VIII* stands under the coaling plant at Coleraine shed in August 1956. Gerry Douglas/courtesy Chris Banks.

W class Mogul No.91 *The Bush*, makes a fine sight leaving Belfast on the 5.35pm service to Portadown on a July afternoon in 1963. The first two carriages are of NCC origin, the next two are GNR K15s in their original livery. Richard Whitford.

NCC VETERANS

Though the Jeeps and Moguls dominated the steam fleet on the NCC lines some older engines survived into our period. Two are illustrated here.

Below: **The V class 0-6-0s were built at Derby in 1923. Despite the strong Midland influence on the design they are the last locomotives in which some observers have been able to detect signs of B&NCR practice. They had 5ft 2½in driving wheels, weighed 47 tons and had a tractive effort of 20,031 lbs. No.13** pictured here was the last of her class and the last NCC 0-6-0 in existence. She finished her career at Belfast York Road where she was restricted to shunting duties. No.13 survived until 1965. She is shunting some wagons with containers behind the large signal box at York Road on 21st May 1963. Greg Child.

Bottom: **The NCC once had an extensive network of lines in mid Ulster. One line ran from Cookstown Junction on the main line, to Cookstown via Toome and Magherafelt. A branch from this line went to Draperstown and a line known as the Derry Central completed the picture, running from Macfin near Coleraine to join the Cookstown line just** outside Magherafelt. The UTA ended passenger services on these lines in 1950 but goods trains survived for some more years. Magherafelt, once the hub of these lines, is the setting for this picture of one of the last NCC 4-4-0s to remain in service. U2 class No.74 *Dunluce Castle* is making up a goods train not long before the cessation of services in 1959. The U2 class introduced in the 1920s, were largely displaced from main line work by the arrival of the Moguls. Ireland's Castle class were named after historic locations around the NCC system. These 4-4-0s bore a strong resemblance to the MR/LMS 4-4-0s used extensively in Britain on their parent company's lines. A. L. Barnett / Colour-Rail.

Above: **No.18 was photographed at York Road on 27th August 1955. This is possibly the only colour photograph of this engine which was withdrawn the following year.** Michael Costeloe.

Right: **No.19 was not withdrawn until 1963; it is seen here shunting at York Road on 10th June 1963.** Greg Child.

JINTIES

Because of the difference in gauge very few locomotives built for service in Britain have been transferred to Ireland; the cost of rebuilding locos to the Irish gauge has normally been prohibitive.

Despite this in 1944 the LMS regauged two of their standard shunting and light freight locos and transferred them to the NCC. Engines of this class were commonly known in Britain as Jinties. The two engines were LMS No.7456, built by Bagnall in 1926 which became NCC No.18 and LMS No.7553 built by Hunslet in 1928 numbered 19 by the

NCC. They were used for general shunting duties and for trip workings on Belfast's quays, being based at York Road.

THE NCC RAILCARS

Right: **The NCC began to experiment with railcars in the 1930s. No.1 was built in 1933. It was powered by two Leyland 130 hp petrol engines and had seats for six first and fifty-five third class passengers. No.1 lasted until the 1960s and is seen here awaiting its next turn in the sidings at York Road.** Harry Luff.

Right lower: **A special type of trailer with a low roof was built for use with railcars Nos 2, 3 and 4. This was to allow the driver to see over the trailer if it was leading. This design feature gave both the railcars and their trailers a noticeably squat appearance. The difference in height between these vehicles and conventional stock is most apparent in this view of one of the trailers in a siding at York Road flanked by two normal sized coaches.** Harry Luff.

Below: **Between 1934 and 1938 three more railcars of a different design to No.1 were introduced. These had diesel engines and their drivers sat in elevated turrets at either end of the cars. This was to allow them to propel trailers without the need to run round at termini. In fact the driver had a restricted view when a trailer was being pushed ahead of the railcar and this practice was stopped when a railcar working in this fashion hit a cow. The turrets remained until the railcars were withdrawn. Railcar No.4 built in 1938 is seen leaving Ballymena on a down stopping service in May 1963.** Greg Child.

THE WT CLASS

The modernisation of the NCC steam fleet begun in the 1930s with the W class Moguls, was completed with the delivery of the eighteen WT class 2-6-4Ts between 1947 and 1950. Known to railwaymen and enthusiasts alike as the 'Jeeps', they were in effect a tank version of the Moguls. The two classes had the same size of driving wheels and cylinders, boiler pressure and tractive effort.

Though based on the Stanier and Fairburn 2-6-4Ts of the LMS, they had distinct NCC features such as cast number plates on their bunkers and smoke box door wheels, which most Irish railways used in preference to the handle favoured by British railways.

The Jeeps were an unqualified success. They were used on every sort of duty all over the NCC system and latterly on the GNR lines taken over by the UTA in 1958. The survivors of the class were the last steam locomotives in regular service in the British Isles and one of the first batch No.4, preserved by the Railway Preservation Society of Ireland, has performed with distinction on railtours all over the island.

Above: **WT class 2-6-4T No.8 stands outside Belfast York Road station in the late 50s beside an advertisement for one of Belfast's most famous products.** Harry Luff.

Above: **WT class No.4 leaves Belfast on the 9.30 am Sunday School special to Portrush on 2nd July 1966. The vehicle behind the loco is a 'brown van'. One or more of these vans, used to convey parcels and luggage, almost always seemed to be in the consist of NCC section trains.** Derek Young.

Above: **When the UTA took over the GNR lines in Northern Ireland the Jeeps were soon to be as familiar there as on their home territory. On 28th August 1965 Nos 6 and 1 simmer quietly in the former goods yard at Lisburn having worked special trains to the town earlier in the day.** Richard Whitford.

Above: **In a bizarre experiment in 1965, one of the Jeeps No.55, was fitted with a tender from an NCC Mogul to increase its water capacity. It worked one or two trips to Dublin in this guise. This, the UTA's great contribution to the development of the steam locomotive, was obviously ahead of its time! The arrangement does not seem to have been widely adopted elsewhere.** Derek Young.

THE UTA AEC RAILCARS

Top: **In 1951 the UTA acquired two railcars Nos 6 and 7, from AEC. A trailer was converted from an existing LMS** designed carriage. **This formed the prototype for the MEDs which were built in quantity in the next few years. The first UTA railcar train is seen on an up service to Belfast at Whiteabby in 1957.** Harry Luff.

Above: **In later years Nos 6 and 7 were transferred to the GNR section where running without a trailer as a two-car unit they were used on local services out of Great Victoria Street. In the early 1960s they were seen on such a duty at Adelaide.** Harry Luff.

THE MULTI PURPOSE DIESELS

Following the success of diesel railcars on the Bangor line the UTA determined to dieselise regular services on the NCC as soon as possible. This was done using the new Multiple Purpose Diesels (MPDs), built between 1957 and 1962. Converted from existing loco hauled stock and variously powered by engines supplied by Leyland, AEC and Rolls-Royce, the MPDs were even used to haul goods trains in the declining years of freight traffic on the UTA.

Right: **A four car MPD set headed by No.55 built in 1959 prepares to form the 1.35pm train to Coleraine from Portrush on 24th April 1962.** Richard Whitford.

Below: **In 1965 the UTA experimented with different colour schemes for the various sections of its railways. In the livery chosen for the NCC lines an MPD set headed by No.63 halts at Ballymoney on the 11.30am service from London-derry to Belfast on 31st July of that year.** Richard Whitford.

THE LARNE LINE

Left: **The railway reached Larne in 1862 from which time steamer services on the short sea crossing to Scotland commenced. These services continue to this day. Larne has two stations, Larne Town and Larne Harbour. WT class 2-6-4T No.3 is seen leaving Larne Harbour on 17th July 1962 with the 7.00pm train to Belfast. The upper quadrant signals at Larne Harbour are the only examples of this type in Ireland. All other semaphore signals in Ireland are of the lower quadrant or somersault varieties.** Richard Whitford.

Lower left: **On 15th July 1966 WT class No.51 hurries the 5.55pm Belfast York Road to Larne Harbour boat train past the staggered platforms of Barn station near Carrickfergus.** Derek Young.

Below: **Steam meets diesel at Ballycarry on the 8th April 1967. WT class No.4 waits in the loop with a permanent way train, for the 11.00am Larne Harbour to Belfast York Road, formed of one of the then new NIR English Electric 70 class railcar sets, to clear the single line section.** Richard Whitford.

THE BACK LINE

Until 1934 all NCC trains from Belfast to Londonderry had to reverse at Greenisland. In that year the loop at Greenisland was constructed, the work having involved the erection of a large reinforced concrete viaduct at Bleach Green. This enabled main line trains to run direct to and from Belfast without the reversal at Greenisland. The original line remained open until the 1960s. Using this line, referred to as the 'back line', trains from Larne could run direct in the direction of Londonderry as required.

Right: **WT class No.2 travels along the 'back line' on 12th July 1963 with the empty coaches to form a special from Ballyclare Junction to Carrickfergus.** Derek Young

Below: **On 3rd June 1967 WT class No.4 is seen climbing from Bleach Green Junction to Monkstown with a special for Portrush. The disconnected junction with the 'back line' can be seen to the left of the locomotive.** Derek Young.

THE PORTRUSH BRANCH

The short branch from Coleraine to Portrush on the North Antrim coast was opened in 1855. A popular destination for holidaymakers and excursionists, special trains regularly brought steam locomotives to the branch after the normal service had been dieselised.

Left: **WT class No.6 with steam to spare heads the 11.15am train from Portrush to Belfast near Portstewart on 17th July 1965. The station for Portstewart was 1¾ miles from the town. From 1882 to 1926 a 3ft gauge roadside steam tramway connected the town and its station. The Portstewart Tramway was one of the first lines in Ireland to close when a bus service was put on in place of the trams in January 1926.** Richard Whitford.

Below: **On 21st July 1962 WT class No.7 heads a return special to Belfast past sister engine No.4 which is waiting to back down to the station to haul a later train.** Richard Whitford.

THE MAIN LINE
TO LONDONDERRY

Above: **WT class No.55 pauses at Antrim
on 21st May 1966 with a Sunday School
excursion which it has just brought up
the branch from the GNR main line at
Knockmore Junction.** Derek Young.

Opposite top: **Though scheduled goods
traffic within Northern Ireland ended in
the mid-60s, the UTA continued to
convey freight from CIE for County
Donegal, to the NCC terminus at
Londonderry whence it was taken on to
its final destination by road. Usually the
CIE freight was hauled overnight by MPD
railcars but problems with these led to
the rare appearance of the CIE freight in
daytime hauled by WT class No.56
substituting for the failed diesels.
The train is seen here near Coleraine on
13th July 1966.** Derek Young.

Right: **WT class No.6 departing from
Coleraine with the 1.00pm Londonderry
to Belfast train, 20th July 1963.**
Richard Whitford.

Below: **Coleraine was the junction for the Portrush branch and an important town in its own right. The Portrush branch diverged just beyond the station. WT class No.7 brings the 3.25pm train off the branch and into Coleraine station on 20th July 1963. The Line diverging to the left just beyond the level crossing was a branch to Coleraine Harbour which closed in 1966.** Richard Whitford.

Below: **Beyond Coleraine the NCC main line follows the picturesque coast line for some miles. A five piece MPD set plus the ubiquitous NCC brown van leaves the seaside town of Castlerock with the 2.55pm Belfast to Londonderry train on 1st June 1963.** Richard Whitford.

Opposite top: **The spirit of the NCC lives on as recently ex-works WT No.6 storms out of Coleraine with the 3.35pm Portrush to Belfast train on 3rd July 1965. The first two vehicles in the train were built by the LMS in the 1930s and were called North Atlantic coaches after the eponymous express for which they were specially constructed.** Derek Young.

Opposite lower: **The NCC station at Londonderry Waterside is the last surviving station in a city which once had four termini. Steam, diesel and CIE freight wagons are seen in this August 1965 view. WT class No.52 is about to depart with the 2.10pm train to Belfast York Road.** Richard Whitford.

THE SPOIL TRAINS

The last steam locomotives to remain in regular service in the British Isles were a handful of Jeeps retained by NIR, the successor to the UTA, to haul stone from a quarry near Larne to construct a motorway along the shores of Belfast Lough parallel to the NCC main line.

Right: **Usually the spoil trains had an engine at each end but on 15th August 1967 a down empty train was double-headed through Whitehead led by WT No.5.** Derek Young.

Below: **At Magheramorne quarry WT No.56 heads a train of spoil wagons being filled at the loading bay, while sister locomotive No.55 which will bank the heavy train, takes water.**
Derek Young.

Right: **The now preserved No.4 heads a loaded spoil train past Bleach Green Halt on 24th March 1967. The embankment on the left carries the NCC main line over the down Larne line which it crosses on Bleach Green viaduct, opened in 1934. At that time it was the longest reinforced concrete viaduct in the British Isles. The building of the viaduct and the new loop which enabled Belfast to Londonderry trains to run direct without reversing at Greenisland, was partly funded by the government of Northern Ireland to help relieve the heavy unemployment of the early 1930s.** Richard Whitford.

Below: **WT No.50 waits in the siding laid along side the NCC main line at Fortwilliam as the spoil is discharged from her train. This part of Belfast has been radically changed by the motorway which the Jeeps helped to construct.** Richard Whitford.

Chapter Two

ON GREAT NORTHERN TRACKS

All those interested in railways have their own particular favourite lines and locomotive types. I have long suspected that childhood memories play a part in the selection of these favourites. The pleasant association of the Great Western Railway with holidays in the West Country, may help to explain the great affection in which that railway is held by so many enthusiasts in England. My railway was the GNR, and this section of the book has been for me, truly a labour of love.

Growing up in the town of Omagh in mid Ulster on the GNR line from Portadown to Derry, invariably referred to by GNR men as, 'the Derry road', many of my earliest childhood memories seem to be linked to the railway. I remember the sadness expressed by my parents when the GNR branch to Bundoran was closed; Sunday excursions to that seaside resort had been part of the life of the town for decades. My first furtive footplate trip was in the cab of a blue engine on a dark winter's evening at Omagh station, and when I acquired my first bicycle a frequent destination was the station and in particular the overbridge just north of it, from where a good view could be obtained of the engine shunting in the goods yard.

Much of the appeal of the GNR was and is an aesthetic one. GNR locomotives were handsome machines with clean lines uncluttered by extraneous plumbing and other bits of equipment. The GNR had been quick to appreciate the necessity of standardisation in its loco fleet and from the 1890s to the end of steam a pattern was set, with 4-4-0s of various designs for passenger trains, and

0-6-0s, often variants of the passenger classes, for freight. The GNR also possessed a small number of tank engines for shunting and short workings around Belfast and Dublin. In a number of instances boilers and other parts were interchangeable between passenger and freight types. The other great distinguishing characteristic of GNR engines was the magnificent sky blue livery which began to appear in the 1930s. From 1948 to the end of the GNRB's existence, it could be seen on most classes of 4-4-0s on the system enhancing already elegant locomotives still further.

The GNR was a large system with, at its greatest extent in 1922, over 600 route miles. Its main line joined Ireland's two largest cities Dublin and Belfast, whilst a secondary main line from Derry joined the Belfast-Dublin route at Portadown. A series of lines collectively known as the Irish North West after the company which had run them until its absorption into the GNR in 1876, meandered from Dundalk to Clones, Enniskillen and Omagh, crossing the border many times along the way. Branches of the GNR served towns in the counties of Antrim, Armagh, Down, Louth and Cavan and one branch reached the Atlantic coast at Bundoran in County Donegal. By Irish standards the GNR had quite intensive suburban services into its Dublin and Belfast termini and its well equipped works at Dundalk provided a high standard of maintenance for both locomotives and the rest of the company's rolling stock.

It must not be forgotten that the GNR was an early pioneer in the field of diesel

traction. From the emergence of Railcar A from Dundalk in 1932 to the end of its independent existence, the GNR developed a series of railcars and railbuses for various duties, culminating in the AEC engined railcars of 1950 which provided some of the first diesel powered express services to run in the British Isles. Painted in an attractive blue and cream livery and fitted for multiple-unit operation, they took over a number of the Dublin-Belfast duties from steam locomotives and were also used on the Irish North Western section and on the line to Derry.

As a footnote to this chapter I have included coverage of that remarkable concern the Sligo, Leitrim & Northern Counties Railway which made a junction with the GNR at Enniskillen.

Independent from its incorporation in 1875 until its closure in 1957, the SL&CR straggled across the bleak and thinly populated border counties in its name and struggled with its balance sheet throughout most of its existence. Surviving latterly on subsidies from the Dublin government and relying heavily on the conveyance of cattle, which were taken on to the east coast ports for shipment to England, by the GNR, it is ironic that the final demise of the SL&NCR came about with the closure of the GNR lines to Enniskillen which robbed the SL&NCR of an outlet for its cattle traffic. In our period, passenger services on the SL&NCR were handled by a railbus and a railcar whilst freight and mixed trains were hauled by the line's 0-6-4 tanks built between 1899 and 1949, but with origins traceable to a Beyer Peacock design going back to 1882.

GREAT NORTHERN LOCOMOTIVE PORTRAITS

Over thirty years after its demise, the GNR is still held in great affection by those interested in railways. I believe that one of the reasons for this is that like the Great Western Railway in Britain, the GNR had a long innings which was not cut short by amalgamation or grouping in the 1920s. The GNR was formed in 1876 through the amalgamation of the north of Ireland's most important railway, the Ulster and a number of smaller concerns. Within a few years the inevitable problems of bringing the disparate locomotive departments together had been accomplished and the decision was taken to build a new works at Dundalk. James Park joined the company as Locomotive Superintendent from the English Great Northern and from that time until the end of steam locomotive production in the 1940s, a distinctive GNRI style of locomotive design was apparent. Some commentators have noted the similarity in style between the two Great Northerns and this undoubtedly stems from Park's tenure at Dundalk. From the first 4-4-0s of the 1880s to the VS class of 1948, GNR locomotives bear a family resemblance as instantly recognisable as that of the GWR across the water.

Continuity was maintained by the fact that the position of Locomotive Superintendent/Chief Mechanical Engineer was held by only five men between 1885 and 1950. The locomotive policy followed by these men was one of steady evolution and quiet progress based on established practice. There was never a GNR 4-6-0 partly because the works would have had difficulty coping with a loco of that size but also in truth because it was never really needed, and though the GNR acquired new steam engines as late as 1948, it would be wrong to assume that the company was doggedly infatuated with steam. The Directors of the GNR had come to realise that the future lay with diesel traction. The development of the diesel railcars from the 1930s bears witness to this. However, the sad fact is that the company and the GNRB never had the resources to develop diesel traction to the extent which they knew was necessary.

THE VS CLASS

The five VS class 4-4-0s built by Beyer Peacock in 1948 were the last express steam locomotives delivered to an Irish railway. They were also probably the last 4-4-0s built anywhere in the world. Designed by H. R. McIntosh, they were based on the V class compounds of the 1930s. The VS class were three cylinder simple expansion engines with 6ft 7in driving wheels and a boiler pressure of 220 lbs per sq in and they were fitted with the same type of Belpaire boiler with which the compounds were reboilered in the 1940s. The ultimate development of the GNR 4-4-0; these were handsome and purposeful engines and it is a tragedy that none of them were preserved.

Below: **The VS class were given the names of Irish rivers. Here renumbered as UTA No.58 (GNR No.208)** *Lagan* **is in the shed yard at the GNR's Dublin terminus on 4th June 1961.** Greg Child.

THE COMPOUNDS

The rebuilding of the Boyne viaduct, completed in 1932, allowed heavier engines to be used on the GNR main line. In the same year the first of the V class Compounds appeared. These three cylinder engines were built by Beyer Peacock, who supplied so many engines to the GNR and other Irish railways over the years. As built they had round topped boilers and were among the first to receive the magnificent lined blue livery. Numbered 83 to 87, they were named after birds of prey. Their introduction allowed a considerable improvement in journey times between Belfast and Dublin.

Right: **V class Compound No.85** *Merlin* **is seen at Dundalk in the summer of 1961. The engine is paired with the tender of one of the VS class. No.85 has been preserved and restored to running order by the Railway Preservation Society of Ireland.** John Edgington.

Below: **No.83** *Eagle* **takes water at Goraghwood on a Dublin to Belfast express in April 1955. This view clearly shows the black and white lining used with the blue livery and the original type of tender with which the Compounds were usually paired.**
Gerry Douglas / courtesy Chris Banks.

THE S CLASS

The eight S class 4-4-0s were built by Beyer Peacock between 1913 and 1915. They were completely rebuilt at Dundalk in 1938/39. In this form they lasted until the 1960s. One of the class No.171 *Slieve Gullion* has been preserved. Named after Irish mountains, as first built their light axle load of 17 tons enabled them to be used on the main line over the Boyne viaduct. With the arrival of the Compounds they began to be employed on other parts of the system and in the 1950s they were a common sight on the Derry road.

Below top: **Once they hauled the crack expresses on this line but S class No.170 *Errigal* is now reduced to taking the 5.43pm local to Lisburn out of Great Victoria Street station in July 1963. At least she retains her GNR blue livery.** Richard Whitford.

Bottom: **Seen at Adelaide on 2nd March 1963, the drab UTA black livery cannot conceal the elegance of UTA No.60 (GNR No.172) *Slieve Donard*.** Richard Whitford.

THE Q CLASS

The Q class and their close relatives the QLs were designed by Clifford and appeared between 1899 and 1910. These typically GNR inside cylindered 4-4-0s were long associated with the Derry road. They were also surprisingly camera shy as far as colour illustrations are concerned at least. One member of the class, No.131, was preserved by CIE at the end of steam operations in the Irish Republic.

Below: **I am most grateful that Greg Child recorded No.132, a member of the Q class acquired by CIE in 1958, on an Irish Railway Record Society special train at Dunboyne, on the ex-MGWR line to Navan and Kingscourt, in June 1961.**

Above: **The last of the 1948 batch of UGs, UTA No.49 (GNR No.149) leaves Bangor with a permanent way train on 10th August 1965.** Derek Young.

THE U & UG CLASSES

The lightweight 4-4-0s of the U class were ideal for use on secondary lines. They were designed by Clifford and were introduced in two batches thirty three years apart. The 1948 batch had some modifications to the original design, notably side window cabs. All of these engines were built by Beyer Peacock. The GNR practice of having 0-6-0 variants of their 4-4-0 classes is illustrated by the UG class which had many components in common with the U class, including boilers and cylinders. The ten UGs were built in two batches, five at Dundalk in 1937 and five by Beyer-Peacock in 1948.

Opposite top: **U class 4-4-0 UTA No.68 (GNR No.205)** *Down* **was the last of the 1948 engines: in UTA black she was at Adelaide in May 1963.** Greg Child.

Opposite bottom: **One of the 1915 engines No.197** *Lough Neagh* **was photographed at Enniskillen in the summer of 1956.** Gerry Douglas / courtesy Chris Banks.

THE PP CLASS

The seventeen engines of the PP class were introduced between 1896 and 1911. They had 6ft 7in drivers and were used across the system, notably on the Irish North West section.

Right: **The GNR crane loco used at Dundalk was a one off supplied by Hawthorn Leslie in 1928. In 1958 it went to CIE and is seen here at Inchicore in 1961.** Michael Costeloe.

Below: **No.75 pictured at Clones in 1956, has the familiar red Beyer Peacock maker's plate on the framing beside the front driving wheel. Not all the 4-4-0s had the blue livery but No.75 looks splendid in her simple unlined black. Strictly speaking No.75 was classified as a PPs locomotive, the small 's' indicated that she had been superheated.**
Gerry Douglas / courtesy Chris Banks.

GNR TANK LOCOMOTIVES

Though not a great user of tank locomotives the most numerous class on the GNR were the T1 and T2 4-4-2Ts, built between 1913 and 1929, which numbered, taken together, 25 engines.

Opposite top: **The RT class 0-6-4Ts were built by Beyer Peacock to the design of Clifford between 1908 to 1911. They were used for shunting mostly in the Belfast area. UTA No.24 (GNR No.166) is engaged in this activity at Adelaide in the early 1960s. Though still with GNR on her tanks she carries her new number on her bunker.** Harry Luff.

Opposite bottom: **One of the last survivors, No.5 was at Great Victoria Street in July 1963. This engine retained the same number under both GNR and UTA ownership.** Richard Whitford.

GOODS ENGINES

Like most Irish railways the GNR favoured 0-6-0s for freight traffic. In our period the 0-6-0s most commonly seen were the UG class which were really mixed traffic engines that could go virtually anywhere with their light axle loading, and the bigger of the SG, SG2 and SG3 classes. Two of the bigger 0-6-0s are illustrated here.

Right: **The SG3s were the most powerful 0-6-0s to run in Ireland. SG3 UTA No.33 (GNR No.20) is on shed at Portadown on 19th July 1962.** Richard Whitford.

Below: **SG2 class UTA No.38 (GNR No.16) is shunting at Belfast on 19th May 1963.** Greg Child.

42

GREAT NORTHERN RAILCARS

The GNR was early in the field of railcar development. The company realised the potential for savings, on lines where traffic was light, using these vehicles. The first railcars emerged from Dundalk in 1932.

Bottom: **Railcar A was a diesel mechanical unit powered by an AEC engine. It was turned out in the blue and cream livery already in use on the GNR's road buses. In this May 1955 view railcar A is at Dundalk.** Michael Costeloe.

Left: **Railcar A went to the UTA in 1958. It was renumbered 101 and painted in UTA green with black and yellow warning stripes at each end. In this guise it is seen at Foyle Road, Derry in July 1962.** Richard Whitford.

Right: **Due to the very light traffic on some passenger lines, the GNR built a series of railbuses which were literally road buses converted to run on rails. They were equipped with the Howden-Meredith patent wheel, the invention of two Dundalk engineers. This combined a steel flange with a pneumatic tyre. Here railbus No.2 (originally numbered F3) dating from 1944, is seen at Dundalk in May 1955 with one of the railbuses which the GNR built for the SL&NCR.** Michael Costeloe.

Lower right: **Railcars D and E appeared in 1936. These had two saloons articulated to a central six wheel section containing the 153hp Gardner power unit. Railcar D, allocated the number 103 by the UTA but retaining its GNR livery, is passing Portadown Junction on 19th July 1962 with the 6.24pm train to Newry. Note the luggage trailer, far left.** Richard Whitford.

Bottom: **The third railcar was a rather different creature from Railcars A and B. Railcar C, later C1, dating from 1934 had its engine and driving compartment separate from and articulated to the passenger saloon. Powered by a 96hp Gardner diesel engine it could only be driven from one end and had to be turned at the end of each journey. Small luggage trailers were constructed to run with the railcars and in this view of C1 at Cavan in the summer of 1956 its trailer can be seen behind the railcar with its lid propped up.** Gerry Douglas / courtesy Chris Banks.

Opposite bottom: **Though an early pioneer of diesel railcars, the GNR had only one diesel locomotive which was supplied to the Board in 1954. This was No.800, an eight wheel diesel hydraulic supplied by the German firm of Maschinenbau A-G of Kiel. In 1958 it went to CIE. In CIE green and renumbered K801 it is seen leaving Cork Glanmire Road on 5th September 1959 with a train for Youghal.** M.Costeloe.

Above: **The ultimate development of the GNR railcar came with the order placed in 1948 with AEC for twenty units which ran in pairs, with an unpowered coach in the middle, as a three car multiple unit. The Park Royal bodies of the power cars seated twelve first and thirty two third class passengers. On of these sets with power cars Nos 616 and 617 was photographed at Enniskillen in 1956.** Gerry Douglas / courtesy Chris Banks

Below: **Shunting in the carriage sidings at Great Victoria Street on 28th August 1965 is SG3 class UTA No.37 (GNR No.97), with WTs Nos 55 and 56 also in attendance. The GNR station was conveniently situated in Belfast's city centre, and although it closed in the 1970s, as this book went to press it seemed increasingly likely that a new station would be built there and the line reopened.** *Richard Whitford.*

Below: **Leaving Belfast's Great Victoria Street station in August 1960 is PPs class 4-4-0 No.42 on the 1.10pm train to Lisburn. This type of locomotive was not often seen on such workings.** *Richard Whitford.*

Below: **Just outside Great Victoria Street the former Belfast Central Railway joined the GNR at Central Junction. On 12th June 1965 UG class UTA No.48 (GNR No.146) brings an excursion from Bangor back onto GNR tracks. If current plans are realised a new triangular junction will be built here and the tracks on the left of the picture leading to Great Victoria Street will be reinstated.**
Derek Young

Below: **At Hilden between Belfast and Lisburn VS class No.207 *Boyne* heads the 9.25am train from Belfast to Dublin on the 3rd of September 1964.** Derek Young.

Top: **28th August 1965 was a busy day at Lisburn. A train of ex-GNR AEC railcars speeds through the staton as WT class 2-6-4T No.56 enters with a special train from the NCC section of the UTA. Its sister No.1 is already in the yard with an earlier arrival. The special trains were run in conjunction with a Royal Black Preceptory demonstration being held in the town that day.** Richard Whitford.

Above: **On August 28th 1965 UG class 0-6-0 UTA No.48 (GNR No.146) arrives at Lurgan with a special from Belfast.** Derek Young.

Right: **WT class No.53 leans on the curve at Hilden near Lisburn with a special train from Belfast to Lurgan on 28th August 1965. The Belfast to Lisburn line was originally built to a gauge of 6ft 2in but relaid in the 1840s to the then new Irish Standard Gauge of 5ft 3in.** Derek Young.

Above: **Goraghwood was the junction for the branch to Newry and Warrenpoint. The continuation of this line to Armagh had closed in 1955. It was also the station where H.M. Customs examined trains. On 25th July 1963 a down goods from Dundalk headed by W class 2-6-0 No.94** *The Maine* **is resuming its northbound progress after customs examination.** Richard Whitford.

Left: **Southbound trains had a stiff climb from Goraghwood up to the summit of the line at milepost 65 ¹⁄₂. Here on a damp and dreary day 5th December 1964, SG3 class UTA No.37 (GNR No.97) struggles up the bank with the 9.05am goods from Portadown to Dundalk.** Derek Young.

Right: **Dundalk, the location of the GNR's works, was also the junction for the Irish North West line. Here on the down side of the main island platform the fireman of WT class No.54 has been at work preparing a good fire for the stiff climb ahead.** John Edgington.

Below: **U class 4-4-0 No.203 *Armagh* in immaculate condition adds a vacuum braked four wheel van to a rake of passenger coaches at Dundalk in May 1957.** F.W.Shuttleworth.

Opposite top: **Northbound trains faced a climb out of the Boyne valley to a summit at Kellystown signal box. On 18th May 1963 VS class UTA No.58 (GNR No.208) *Lagan* is working hard with a train for Belfast.** Greg Child.

Opposite bottom: **The branch to Ardee which opened in 1896 diverged from the main line at Dromin Junction south of Dundalk. Ardee lost its passenger service in the 1930s but the branch remained open for freight until the 1970s. A GNR 0-6-0 has the road for the main line with the branch freight.** John Edgington.

THE HOWTH BRANCH

The short branch from Howth Junction to Howth always had a significant commuter traffic into Dublin. For many years GNR T class 4-4-2Ts were used on the line.

Below: **4-4-2T No.66 is leaving Howth with a train for the city in the late 50s. The first coach on the train is one of a number which the GNR acquired of L&NWR origin. The narrower profile of this vehicle built to the English loading gauge is apparent from this angle.** F. W. Shuttleworth.

Bottom: **The GNR articulated railcars were commonly used on the line. Railcar G enters the one intermediate station on the branch in GNR days, Sutton and Baldoyle, with a train for Dublin.** Gerry Douglas / courtesy Chris Banks.

Above: **Ex-GNR railcars headed by No.608 in CIE black and orange livery arrive at Sutton and Baldoyle on 18th May 1963.** Greg Child.

Above: **Railcar F waits at Howth station to form a return service to Amiens Street. In the 1980s the Howth branch was electrified as part of the Dublin Area Rapid Transit System and smart green German built electric units now perform the duties once undertaken by GNR tank engines and railcars.** F.W.Shuttleworth.

AMIENS STREET SHED

The former GNR shed at Amiens Street was the last steam shed in Dublin. In the declining years of steam it played host to some unusual visitors. The building is still in use today, being used to service and maintain CIE diesel locomotives.

Right: **Built by the GS&WR in 1900, D11 class 4-4-0 No.301 was on shed at Amiens Street on 13th July 1961. This loco was withdrawn the following year.**
Richard Whitford.

Below: **NCC Moguls made it to Dublin in the 1960s. On Saturday 7th December 1963 No.97 *Earl of Ulster* is on Amiens Street shed in the company of VS class No.207 *Boyne.* Derek Young.**

54

THE DERRY ROAD

The GNR route from Belfast to Derry was longer than the NCC line and more difficult to work but it served the towns and villages of mid Ulster well for over one hundred years, until its destruction in 1965 by the overtly anti-railway government of Northern Ireland. The Derry road left the main line at Portadown Junction.

Left: **SG class UTA No.43 (GNR No.175) heads west from the junction with a goods for Omagh on 19th July 1962.** Richard Whitford.

Below: **Dungannon was the first important town on the line. It was also the junction for the branch to Cookstown which lost its passenger services in 1956. On 19th July 1962 U class UTA No.67 (GNR No.202)** *Louth* **is about to leave Dungannon with the 4.40pm local to Portadown.** Richard Whitford.

Top: **Omagh was my home town and I spent many happy hours watching trains in the environs of the station. On 20th June 1962, the driver of W class 2-6-0 No.91 *The Bush* surrenders the single line tablet to the signalman at Omagh South Box. The train is the 1.35pm arrival from Belfast. The line to the right, now reduced to a siding, led to Enniskillen and Bundoran until its closure in 1957.** Richard Whitford.

Above: **Goods traffic at Omagh was healthy judging from the number of wagons in the yard. In this view SG3 UTA No.40 (GNR No.18) is shunting there on 20th July 1962. In addition to the goods sidings at the station, the GNR had a separate goods depot at Omagh in the Market Yard, served by a branch which joined the line to Portadown about one mile south of the passenger station.** Richard Whitford.

Opposite top: **WT class No.57, the last one built, is turned beside the disused and roofless engine shed at Omagh on 31st August 1964 before working the 5pm train back to Belfast. The site of the station, goods and engine sheds and much of the trackbed through the town has been lost to that mark of 'civilisation' - the by-pass! The local council plan to name the route 'Great Northern Road' in a fitting tribute to the old company.** Derek Young.

Above: **Strabane was where the GNR made contact with the County Donegal narrow gauge lines. In this 1956 view S class No.174 *Carrantuohill* is leaving the station with a Derry to Belfast train. The footbridge in the background led on to the narrow gauge station.** Harry Luff.

Right: **The GNR terminus at Foyle Road, Derry, was on a cramped site next to the river.** Richard Whitford.

Above: **The Harbour Commissioners employed steam locomotives to work their lines. These were unusual in that they had draw gear for both the 3ft and 5ft 3in gauges, though they could only haul wagons of one gauge at a time. One of these engines is preserved in Belfast Transport Museum, while another, No.3 *R.H.Smyth*, a 1928 Avonside Engine Company 0-6-0 saddle tank, works no. 2021, is in the care of the Railway Preservation Society of Ireland. It is here seen giving train rides at the Society's Whitehead base.** Charles Friel.

THE LONDONDERRY PORT AND HARBOUR COMMISSIONERS

At one time the city of Derry had four railway stations, two on each bank of the River *Foyle* which divides the city. One on each bank was broad gauge and one was narrow gauge. On the east side of the river were the terminus of the NCC line from Belfast and the Victoria Road station of the branch of the CDR narrow gauge which ran down the Northern Ireland side of the *Foyle* from Strabane. On the other bank was the terminus of the GNR Derry road and, some way out of the city centre was the station of the Londonderry & Lough Swilly Railway at Graving Dock.

These stations and gauges were connected by the system of dock lines and tramways operated by the Londonderry Port and Harbour Commissioners. These tracks were mixed gauge. The Commissioners' lines ran across the bottom deck of Londonderry's Craigavon Bridge. Locos were not permitted and wagons were taken across the river by means of capstans and wagon turntables.

Right: **The complicated arrangements required for mixed gauge track are illustrated in this 1962 view taken on the quays on the west bank of the river. It also shows the difference between the 5ft 3in and the 3ft gauges.** Richard Whitford.

THE NEWRY AND WARRENPOINT LINE

This line joined the Belfast to Dublin line at Goraghwood. Between Warrenpoint and Newry it closely followed the shores of Carlingford Lough; beyond Newry it climbed steeply up to Goraghwood. The line closed in 1965 but Newry is now served by a new NIR station on the main line.

Above: **On 21st July 1963 U class UTA No.68 (GNR No.205)** *Down* **leaves Newry Edward Street station with the 4.10pm Warrenpoint to Goraghwood train.** Richard Whitford.

Left: **On Friday September 23rd 1963 the 2.15pm goods from Newry is nearing Goraghwood. The train is headed by S class UTA No.63 (GNR No.192)** *Slievenamon* **which in its heyday would have been in charge of the best trains on the main line and not the branch goods.** Derek Young.

On 22nd June 1962 UG class 0-6-0 UTA No.45 (GNR No.78) passes Narrow Water Castle with the 4.10pm Warrenpoint to Goraghwood train. Richard Whitford.

At Warrenpoint five years after the end of the GNRB, a GNR loco heads a GNR train from a typically Great Northern station. UG class UTA No.45 (GNR No.78) is about to depart with an afternoon train in March 1963. Greg Childs.

THE IRISH NORTH WEST

The lines west of Dundalk serving Clones, Cavan and Enniskillen had been operated up to the formation of the GNR in the 1870s, by the Irish North Western Railway Company. The nineteenth century name was unofficially perpetuated in the twentieth century as these lines were often referred to as the Irish North West. Serving areas with small populations and relatively little industry, traffic patterns on these lines were severely disrupted by the partition of Ireland in the 1920s, the border intersecting the railway at numerous points. For example on the fifteen mile section between Clones and Cavan, both of which were in the Republic of Ireland, the railway entered Northern Ireland at two locations. These GNR routes made a junction with the Cavan & Leitrim narrow gauge system at Belturbet and at Cavan they met a branch of the former MGWR railway which came north from the main Dublin to Sligo line at Inny Junction. Motive power on the Irish North West was predominantly the light 4-4-0s of P, PP and U classes. Railcars were also often used. Cattle traffic formed an important part of the freight business. The unilateral decision of the Northern government to close the parts of these lines within their jurisdiction left CIE with no option but to follow suit and shut down the rump left in the Republic; thus was a large part of the north of Ireland left without the benefit of railway communication after 1957.

Top right: **Clones was an important junction with lines radiating in four directions. In April 1956 GNR U class No.202 *Louth*, heads the 9.00am Dublin to Enniskillen train.** John Edgington.

Centre right: **Named trains were uncommon in Ireland but the meandering cross country lines of the Irish North West had one, the *Bundoran Express*. This ran from Dublin to the seaside resort of Bundoran in County Donegal. Popular with holiday makers, the train was also used by pilgrims going to the religious centre of Lough Derg which was not far from Pettigo station on the Bundoran branch. The term express was perhaps a little euphemistic for this train which took about five hours to cover its 160 mile journey. U class No.205 *Down*, on the return journey to Dublin, is at Clones in the summer of 1956.** Gerry Douglas / courtesy Chris Banks.

Fintona, famous for its horse tram which can be seen in the background in this view taken on 30th April 1955 (see Chapter 4), was typical of the small rural communities served by the Irish North West lines. P class 4-4-0 No.73 deals with the branch's modest goods traffic. Gerry Douglas / courtesy Chris Banks.

Enniskillen, the county town of Fermanagh, had services to Omagh, Dundalk, Belfast and Bundoran. Two of the 1915 batch of Us are seen at its station. The first five engines of the U class built in 1915 did not receive names until 1949/50 when they were named after Irish loughs. Top is No.197 *Lough Neagh* and bottom is No.198 *Lough Swilly*. Gerry Douglas / courtesy Chris Banks.

Ballyhaise, on the line from Clones to Cavan, was the junction for the short 4½ mile branch to Belturbet where the GNR shared a station with the C&L narrow gauge line from Dromod. In this delightful sequence photographed by the late Gerry Douglas in August 1956 we are able to relive some of the comings and goings at the station on that sunny summer's day so long ago.

Above: **The branch train, comprising one van and one clerestory coach, waits for the connecting service. The branch engine is No.107, a PPs class 4-4-0.** Gerry Douglas / courtesy Chris Banks.

Above: **The train from Clones to Cavan duly turns up formed of railcar C1 and a luggage trailer.** Gerry Douglas / courtesy Chris Banks.

Above: **The very essence of the old GNR is captured in this picture of P class No.26 about to leave Cavan on a train to Clones in August 1956. Such timeless scenes as these would soon be swept away for ever.** Gerry Douglas / courtesy Chris Banks.

Above: **Later in the day P class No.26, one of the oldest engines still in service dating from the 1890s, waits at Ballyhaise, with a Cavan to Clones train, for the connection off the branch.** Gerry Douglas / courtesy Chris Banks.

Above: **No.107 waits at Belturbet with a return service to Ballyhaise. The narrow gauge line came into the other end of the station on the right hand side of the platform beyond the splendid train shed.** Gerry Douglas / courtesy Chris Banks.

Above: **The usual motive power for the Belturbet branch was the little JT class 2-4-2Ts. No.91 takes over the branch train at Ballyhaise from No.107 which will now presumably go back to Clones shed.** Gerry Douglas / courtesy Chris Banks.

THE SLIGO, LEITRIM AND NORTHERN COUNTIES RAILWAY

Much has been written about that most singular of Irish railways, the SL&NCR. It became the last independent standard gauge railway company in the British Isles by dint of its peculiar geographic position. Because its route straddled the border it escaped the clutches of the GSR in 1925 and the UTA in 1948, and because its finances were so shaky its benign neighbour the GNR was never really interested in acquiring it. The SL&NCR linked the MGWR at Sligo to the GNR at Enniskillen. The SL&NCR line proper ended at Collooney in County Sligo but the company had running powers over the MGWR to Sligo and on that company's branch to Sligo quay. At Collooney it also made a junction with the erstwhile Waterford, Limerick and Western Railway which was taken over by the GS&WR in 1901. At one time this little village had three railway stations.

The area which the railway served was one of the poorest and most sparsely populated parts of Ireland. The lifeblood of the line was cattle which were conveyed in large numbers for onward transit, mostly through Enniskillen, to the east coast ports. When the Northern Ireland government closed the GNR lines to Enniskillen in 1957, the SL&NCR had no outlet for this traffic and no option but to put an end to its operations.

Much of the charm of the SL&NCR was in its rolling stock. Over the years most of its locomotives were 0-6-4Ts supplied by Beyer Peacock. The basic design went back to 1882 and was modified over the years. The first five were delivered between 1882 and 1899. A second batch of three arrived between 1904 and 1917 and finally and perhaps surprisingly two more were ordered in 1947. Having placed the order the company could not afford to pay for them and they were eventually supplied on hire purchase by Beyer Peacock in 1951. With the exception of Bulleid's Turfburner, these were the last steam locomotives supplied to an Irish railway. SL&NCR engines did not have numbers, they were identified by name only. The 1951 locomotives were called *Lough Melvin* and *Lough Erne* and were bought by the UTA when the line closed. Given the numbers 26 and 27 by their new owners they were used for shunting at Belfast. No.27 *Lough Erne* was happily saved for preservation and is in the care of the RPSI.

The SL&NCR followed the lead of the GNR in using railbuses and railcars for its modest passenger traffic. Two railbuses were supplied by the GNR in the 1930s. Known as A and 2A they proved most useful. They could haul a lighweight trailer for luggage and parcels. In 1947 a diesel railcar was ordered from Walkers of Wigan who had made similar vehicles for the CDR. The power unit was articulated from the passenger saloon and the railcar could be driven from either end thus avoiding the need to turn it at the end of a journey as was the case with the railbuses. Railcar B, as it was known, was bought by CIE when the line closed.

Below: **The oldest and the most recent types of SL&NCR locos are seen together at Manorhamilton in 1956. Out of use in the siding is *Lissadell* dating from 1899, while *Lough Erne* shunts her train.**
Gerry Douglas / Chris Banks.

Below: *Lough Erne* at the line's headquarters Manorhamilton in 1956, heading a goods train. Gerry Douglas / courtesy Chris Banks.

Below: **In May 1963 under UTA ownership, No.27 *Lough Erne* is at Whitla Street goods yard in Belfast.** Greg Child.

Two views of railbus 2A. Top: **Complete with its diminutive trailer it sits on the turntable at Enniskillen.** Bottom: **2A pauses hopefully for passengers at Manorhamilton.** Both Gerry Douglas / courtesy Chris Banks.

Below: **The 1947 built railcar B stands outside the small SL&NCR shed at Enniskillen. The end facing the camera contains the power unit. In the background is one of the GNR's AL class 0-6-0s No.56. This loco built at Dundalk in 1896, was originally named *Omagh*, and was not withdrawn until 1960.** Gerry Douglas / courtesy Chris Banks.

Below: **Our last glimpse of the SL&NCR is of railcar B at Sligo station before departure to Enniskillen on 29th May 1957.** F.W.Shuttleworth.

Chapter Three

THE CIE SYSTEM

The standard gauge railways of the Irish Republic underwent a remarkable transformation in the 1950s and in particular in the period between 1955 and 1959. What happened was nothing short of a radical renewal of the system. With hindsight the action that was taken at that time probably saved the railways from being marginalised in terms of their role in the country's transport infrastructure.

The Republic's railways had been starved of funds during the GSR era and it showed. While the railways were a veritable paradise for visiting enthusiasts it was extremely difficult to provide any kind of acceptable service with such obsolete equipment. Much of the stock inherited by the GSR in 1925 was still in everyday use when CIE was formed. In 1949 as many as 83 classes were represented in the CIE fleet of less than 500 steam locomotives.

The arrival of 60 diesel railcars in 1952 and more than 100 diesel locomotives in 1955 and 1956 signalled the onset of modernisation with a vengeance. These coupled to the acquisition of a considerable amount of modern coaching stock all but changed the face of Ireland's railways in a few short years. Despite the new rolling stock much of interest from the steam age survived into our period. Line closures were not as

drastic or as foolhardy in the Republic as in Northern Ireland, and branch and secondary lines saw out the working lives of many venerable steam locomotives. The ubiquitous J15 class was seen throughout the system, some of the J15s retaining their saturated boilers to the end. Some members of the G2 class, the last broad gauge 2-4-0 tender engines in the British Isles, carried on to the end of steam, and examples of the locomotives designs of such famous engineers as Aspinall, H. A. Ivatt and Maunsell, who learned their trade in Ireland before achieving much greater recognition in England, were still to be seen on the CIE system in this period.

This was a fascinating era when the new diesels shared the tracks with the very steam locomotives they were intended to supplant. Some branch services were operated by that increasing rarity, the mixed train conveying both passenger carriages and freight vehicles. On some lines the new C class diesels could be seen hauling ancient bogie and even six wheel coaches. It is a sobering thought that some of the diesel classes which replaced steam are already extinct and I am sure that some readers will find the photographs of the CIE diesels in their early silver and green liveries just as nostalgic as those of the steam locomotives they displaced.

In identifying CIE steam locomotives I have used the system of classification adopted by the GSR in 1925. This was similar to that used by the London & North Eastern Railway in Britain. The first letter denotes the wheel arrangement, for example J indicates an 0-6-0. The numbers that follow show the class of engine within that wheel arrangement; the classification does not distinguish between tank and tender engines. Whilst not much used by railway workers in practice, the GSR system will probably be more comprehensible to readers of this book than the multiplicity of designations used by the constituent companies of the GSR and it remained in official use on CIE until the end of steam.

The three main Dublin stations were given the names of founding fathers of the Irish Republic in 1966. As this came at the end of our period I have used the original names of the stations; thus the present day Connolly, Pearse and Heuston are referred to as Amiens Street, Westland Row and Kingsbridge respectively.

THE 800 CLASS

The only logical beginning for a survey of CIE steam is with the 800 class, the Queens of Ireland's railways. In the context of what the GSR had produced in the way of locomotives between 1925 and 1939, which in truth was not very much, the building of these machines is remarkable. The only steam locomotives built by the GSR up to then had been the Woolwich Moguls, the first of which had in any case been ordered by the MGWR, the 700 series, supposed improvements on the old J15 class, a one off 2-6-2T No.850 and some 0-6-2Ts for the Dublin suburban services and a few additional 4-4-0s of type going back to the days of the GS&WR.

The 800s or to give their official designation, class B1a, were the largest and most powerful steam locomotives ever to run in Ireland. In working order they weighed 84 tons and had a tractive effort of 33,000 lbs. They were among the largest 4-6-0s ever built in the British Isles. In terms of size and power they ranked with the LMS *Royal Scots* and the GWR *Kings*. The three engines were named after legendary Queens from Irish mythology *Meadhbh* (pronounced 'Maeve'), *Macha* and *Tailte*. They never really had the chance to give more than a hint of what they were capable of. Only 800 was in traffic when war between Britain and Nazi Germany broke out in 1939. The then Irish Free State was neutral in the conflict and Britain had little coal to spare for a neutral state. When coal was available it was of very poor quality and the GSR had to struggle to maintain any sort of service at all. Fast schedules and prime performance from the 800 class were completely out of the question. In the post war decade before the arrival of the diesels further problems with coal supply and undemanding schedules denied the class the opportunity to demonstrate consistently what they were capable of achieving. No.802 *Tailte* was withdrawn in 1957, No.801 *Macha* lasted into the early 1960s and No.800 was saved for preservation.

A detail of No.800's nameplate. Greg Child.

Above: **On a murky day at Amiens Street shed the apogees of Great Northern and Great Southern steam stand together. No.800 is on her way north for preservation in Belfast Transport Museum, VS class No.207 *Boyne* was still at work but sadly would be withdrawn the following year and was not to escape the cutter's torch.** Derek Young.

71

Above: **No.801 *Macha* is on a special train at Mallow on 5th June 1961.** Michael Costeloe.

Above: **No.800 at Adelaide in Belfast before she entered the Museum. On her journey north No.800 and the diesel which was hauling her had to be separated by a string of wagons when crossing the Boyne viaduct at Drogheda to reduce the strain on the bridge.** Greg Child.

GREAT SOUTHERN ENGINES

Two of the classes introduced by the GSR are illustrated here.

Right: **The 700 class were supposed to be an improvement on the J15s but were generally reckoned by railwaymen to be weaker engines than the originals. The second batch, of which No.719 pictured here at Mullingar in June 1961 was one, had superheated boilers similar to those used on rebuilds of the J15s themselves.** Greg Child.

Below: **The 0-6-2T wheel arrangement was not often used on the Irish 5ft 3in gauge. The GSR built five of these attractive looking machines for use on the former Dublin & South Eastern suburban lines. I3 class No.673 is seen on shed at Amiens Street on 4th June 1961.** Greg Child.

A DUBLIN & SOUTH EASTERN SURVIVOR

Below: **Very few D&SER engines survived into our period. One that did and which has subsequently been preserved was K2 class 2-6-0 No.461 built by Beyer Peacock in 1922. She was at Dungarvan on the now closed line from Mallow to Waterford on a special train on June 6th 1961. The CIE logo on her tender was often referred to as the 'flying snail'. No.461 and her sister No.462 were designed by the D&SER locomotive engineer G.H.Wild. Delivered at the height of the 'troubles' of the early 1920s which affected the D&SER particularly badly, both engines were sent to Belfast for safe keeping until the situation in the south had calmed down. The two Moguls were used for most of their career on the Wexford goods trains.** Greg Child.

THE J15s

The steam fleet of CIE and before it, that of the GSR and of the GS&WR was dominated by one class of engine which first appeared in 1866, the GS&WR 101 class, the J15s of the GSR. The work of Alexander McDonnell, Locomotive Superintendent of the GS&WR from 1864 to 1883, no less than 111 of the class were built between 1866 and 1903. Few locomotives anywhere in the world can have had such long and useful lives as the J15s. Though originally intended for goods traffic, they were used on all sorts of duties short of express passenger trains. The J15s were much rebuilt over the years and many were latterly given superheated boilers; however some of the class retained their saturated boilers and outside sprung tenders until the end of steam, making them quite a contrast with the modern disels with which they shared the tracks in the late 1950s. Two J15s, Nos.184 and 186, have been preserved. No.184 has the older round topped saturated boiler while No.186 has the superheated Belpaire boiler.

Opposite top: **The class leader No.101 is seen at Patrickswell near Limerick on 25th June 1959 with the mixed train for the Foynes branch. She has acquired a superheated Belpaire boiler, though just how much of the original 1866 engine is left at this stage in her career, is open to debate.** Michael Costeloe.

Opposite bottom: **J15 No.125 at Limerick station in June 1961 with a service for Limerick Junction. The rolling stock of the train is about seventy five years younger than its locomotive.** John Edgington.

Top left: **A decidedly Victorian scene recorded in June 1959. J15 No.131 retains a saturated boiler and outside sprung tender. She is hauling an elderly ex-MG&WR six wheeled coach and a gas tank past Banteer Junction on the line from Mallow to Tralee.** Michael Costeloe.

Bottom left: **Limerick shed was able to carry out quite extensive repairs and overhauls. In June 1959 an early J15 No.109 is receiving attention there.** Michael Costeloe.

Below: **In very poor external condition but judging by the exhaust still in good heart, J15 No.138 blasts away from Portarlington with a ballast train on 11th July 1960.** Greg Child.

Above: **J15 No.170 shunting at Limerick 25th June 1959.** Michael Costeloe.

77

ON SHED AT GLANMIRE ROAD

Glanmire Road shed in Cork usually offered an interesting collection of engines in steam days.

Opposite top: **Ex-MGWR J26 0-6-0T No.560 was constructed in the 1890s to the designs of Martin Atock. They were the standard shunting tank locomotives on the MGWR system and the last examples survived into the 1960s. Next to the little tank engine is one of the K1 class Woolwich Moguls No.385.**
Michael Costeloe

Opposite bottom: **B2a class 4-6-0 No.402 was designed by E. A. Watson, who came to the GS&WR from the GWR. Alas despite the designer's pedigree these were no *Saints* or *Stars*. Originally a four cylinder engine, 402 was drastically rebuilt in the late 1920s with new frames, wheels and only two cylinders. In this form 402 was a success, indeed her rebuild probably saved her as some of her sisters were scrapped at the time of her reconstruction.** Michael Costeloe.

Right: **By 1961 steam had virtually disappeared from the shed as the last of the Bandon tanks No.464 was prepared to work a railtour in March of that year.** Michael Costeloe.

Below: **B4 class 4-6-0T No.470 was one of a class of eight locomotives built by Beyer Peacock for the Cork, Bandon and South Coast Railway between 1906 and 1920. The 4-6-0T was an extremely unusual wheel arrangement on the standard gauge in the British Isles. No.470, pictured here in September 1959, was the only one of the class not to have been rebuilt with a superheated boiler.** Michael Costeloe.

THE J9 CLASS

Right: **The large 0-6-0s of the J9 class were introduced by Coey in 1903. The first of the class No.351 is seen on shed at Waterford in June 1961.** Greg Child.

Below: **In September 1959 J9 class No.252 is about to leave Cork with a train for Youghal. The first coach is of GNR origin.** Michael Costeloe.

EX GS&WR ENGINES

Right: **The little J30 class engines, of which only three were built, were inteded for lightly constructed branch lines in Cork and Kerry. No.100 pictured here at Cork in 1959 displays a very antiquated smokebox door which opens in two halves. One of this engine's sisters, No.90 has been preserved.** Michael Costeloe.

Below: **No.301 was built by Coey in 1900 for express passenger duties. This D11 class 4-4-0 was originally named *Victoria.* She is seen at Amiens Street shed in Dublin in June 1961.** Greg Child.

ASPINALL, IVATT AND MAUNSELL LOCOMOTIVES

Three locomotive engineers who later went on to achieve notable success with major British railway companies had previously worked for the GS&WR at Inchicore. Some of the engines they built in Ireland lasted almost to the end of steam.

Below: **D14 class 4-4-0 No.64 was built by H. A. Ivatt to the design of his predecessor J.A.F.Aspinall. Aspinall left the GS&WR in 1886 for the Lancashire & Yorkshire Railway where he achieved considerable fame and eventually was awarded a knighthood. No.64 was photographed in September 1957 on an Irish Railway Record Society special at Baltinglass on the long branch from Sallins to Tullow which closed completely in March 1959.**
Michael Costeloe.

Above: **R. E. L. Maunsell was at Inchicore from 1911 to 1913. One of the few locos he produced was L2 class 0-4-2 saddletank** *Sambo* **which for decades was the works shunter at Inchicore, where it was photographed in June 1961.** Greg Child.

82

Above: **H. A. Ivatt is best remembered for his work on the English Great Northern to which he moved in 1896 after a ten year stint at Inchicore. The Ivatt Atlantics of the GNR (E) were among the most outstanding locomotives of the Edwardian era. His work in Ireland was on a more modest scale. He continued to build Aspinall's 4-4-0s and the 101 class 0-6-0s of McDonnell. Two original Ivatt designs are shown here. J11 class 0-6-0T No.207 dated from 1887. It is seen out of use at Mallow in June 1959 complete with its archaic smokebox door.** Michael Costeloe.

Below: **The six locos of the F6 class 2-4-2Ts were built between 1892 and 1894. These handsome tanks were used for many years on local trains out of Cork to Cobh and Youghal. No.42 is shunting at Inchicore works on 13th September 1958.** Michael Costeloe.

THE WOOLWICH MOGULS

R.E.L Maunsell left the GS&WR in 1913 to take up the position of Locomotive Engineer on the South Eastern & Chatham Railway. His influence on Irish railways was exerted much more strongly by a class of locomotives which he designed for the SE&CR in 1917 than by anything he did when in charge at Inchicore.

His first design for his new employers was the N class 2-6-0. These proved to be useful engines which lasted until near the end of steam on British Railways' Southern Region in the 1960s. At the end of the 1914-1918 war the British government authorised the building of one hundred locos of this design at Woolwich Arsenal in London for sale to whoever might want them. This was an attempt to keep in employment in peacetime, workers who had been making munitions during the war. In 1923 the MGWR ordered twelve sets of parts of these engines from Woolwich. The first of these kits was assembled at the MGWR Broadstone works in Dublin in 1923 though not actually put to work before the formation of the GSR in 1925. The GSR ordered another fifteen engines in kit form. They were designated the K1 class and given the numbers 372-391. Six later engines had 6ft driving wheels as opposed to 5ft 6in wheels on the earlier locos. These were identical to Maunsell's U class locos built for the Southern Railway in the late 1920s.

In all the MGWR and the GSR bought twenty seven sets of parts though only twenty six locos ever appeared. The most notable difference between the GSR engines and their British cousins was the absence of smoke deflectors on Irish engines. The Woolwich Moguls were used all over the system by the GSR and CIE but particularly on the ex-MGWR lines and on the boat trains from Cork to Rosslare.

84

MGWR ENGINES

The standard goods engine on the Midland system was Martin Atock's 0-6-0 design which was built between 1876 and 1895. Over forty of these were taken into GSR stock in 1925 being designated classes J18 and J19 to distinguish between those engines with round topped and Belpaire boilers. Like the J15s of the GS&WR these were long lived maids of all work.

Opposite: **K1 class No.388 and D12 class 4-4-0 No.307 prepare to take the evening train from Cork to Rosslare in April 1956. Immediately beyond the confines of Cork's Glanmire Road station is the 1,355 yard tunnel, one of the longest on an Irish railway. The stiff 1 in 60-70 gradient through the tunnel made double-heading out of Cork common in the days of steam.**
John Edgington / Colour-Rail.

Opposite below: **Near the end of its days K1 class No.376 is seen on an enthusiasts special at Amiens Street station in Dublin.** John Edgington.

Above: **J19 No.603 was pictured at Limerick Junction in June 1961.** John Edgington.

Below: **The J19s were often used on branch passenger trains. No.599 is on the 8.57 train to Ballinrobe at Claremorris on 24th June 1959.**
Michael Costeloe.

THE LAST 2-4-0s

The last 2-4-0 tender engines in service in the British Isles and probably in Europe were the G2 class. Built by Atock for the MGWR in the 1890s, they had 5ft 8in driving wheels, boiler pressure of 160lbs per sq. in. and were superheated. They were reputed to be capable of speeds in the region of 70mph.

Top: **One of the last haunts of the class was the Ballaghadereen branch in County Roscommon where No.655 (MGWR No.29 *Clonsilla*) was seen outside the single road shed for the branch engine, on 8th June 1961.** Greg Child.

Above: **In the summer of 1956 G2 class 2-4-0 No.659 (MGWR No.13 *Rapid*) is shunting vans and postal vehicles at Sligo. The six wheel postal van next to the engine is of MGWR origin and of roughly the same vintage as No.659.** F.W.Shuttleworth.

THE COMING
OF THE DIESELS

The diesel era on CIE began quietly with the construction in 1947-1948 of small class of diesel shunters at Inchicore. These were followed by an order for two Sulzer engined Bo-Bos for main line service, but with the Milne report suggesting that diesels were not going to be cost effective in Ireland the process of dieselisation slowed for a time. The first widespread manifestation of diesel power came with the order for sixty AEC engined railcars, similar to those in use on the GNR, which began to appear in 1951. The first railcars went into service on the line from Kingsbridge to Waterford and were soon to be seen all over the network.

Below left: **Railcar No.2613 at the former CB&SCR terminus of Cork Albert Quay in May 1956.** John Edgington.

Below: **O. V. Bulleid who came to CIE from the English Southern Railway designed some odd looking railcars which went into service in 1956. Nos 2660-5 were built at Inchicore and though identical to the other railcars in mechanical terms, they were four inches higher than the others and had a rather ugly flat front which did nothing to enhance their appearance. The Bulleid railcars were later converted to powered intermediates. In their original condition one of these vehicles is seen at Kingsbridge in 1957.** Harry Luff.

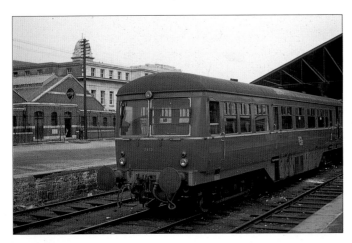

Above: **In John Edgington's lovely panorama of the freight yards at Dublin's North Wall in 1956, D303 one of the 1947/48 Inchicore built diesel shunters is making up a freight train. The yard in the foreground was owned formerly by the L&NWR, that on the top right was the MGWR yard. The LNWR had its own passenger station to serve its cross channel steamers and although passenger trains were withdrawn in the 1920s part of the L&NWR station, a platform and its canopy, may be seen in the centre background of the picture.**

THE A CLASS

The first of the main line diesels began to be delivered in 1955. These were the Co-Co diesel electrics built by Metropolitan Vickers and known on CIE as the A class. Powered by 1,200hp Crossley engines they were quickly put to work on the services from Dublin to Cork and Limerick. The diesels were turned out in a silver grey livery which was ill suited to withstand the rigours of the Irish weather. Over 35 years later many of the A class are still in service on passenger and freight trains throughout the CIE system.

Below: **A17 was less than a year old when seen on 26th April 1956 on the 1.00pm train to Cork at Youghal station.** John Edgington.

Bottom: **The A class quickly came to dominate the main line services from Dublin to the south and west. A38 is pictured on such a duty at Ballybrophy in the summer of 1956.** Gerry Douglas / courtesy Chris Banks.

Below: **The A class were used on goods as well as passenger trains. A14 is making up a freight train composed of loose coupled wagons at Westport in County Mayo in August 1962. This traditional type of goods train is now but a memory. Today's freight services are composed of modern continuously braked wagons capable of running at speeds not far short of those of express passenger trains.** John Edgington.

Bottom: **The silver livery did not wear at all well and locos soon began to appear in a new green colour scheme. A7 is in the new livery at Kingsbridge on 28th August 1960 at the head of the 9.45am express to Cork, the oil lamps on the front would look more at home on a J15 than on a modern diesel.** Michael Costeloe.

THE C CLASS

CIE ordered thirty four 550hp Bo-Bo diesel electrics from Metropolitan Vickers at the same time as the order for the A class was placed. These C class diesels also had Crossley engines. They were similar in appearance to the A class but were 9ft shorter. Intended for branch and secondary duties they were rather underpowered and in any case many of the lines for which they were designed were soon to close.

Top: **The C class soon began to get the green livery. On 11th July 1961 C class No.211 heads for the goods yard at Cork Glanmire Road with a long van train for such a small locomotive.** Richard Whitford.

Opposite bottom: **The changeover from steam to diesel is poignantly illustrated by this scene at Waterford shed in June 1961. The remains of the Aspinall designed D17 class 4-4-0 No.3 dating from 1883 rust quietly in the background as the new order on CIE is represented by C class No.227.** John Edgington.

Above: **On the sort of duty for which they were intended, C210 stands at the terminus of the Clonakilty branch in County Cork in May 1958 with the branch train of one van and a single bogie coach.** John Edgington.

BRITISH AND GERMAN DIESELS

Right: **Less well known than the A and C classes was the small class of A1A-A1A Sulzer engined diesels supplied in 1955. One of these is arriving at Birdhill on the Limerick to Nenagh and Ballybrophy line in June 1961. B109 graphically illustrates the state to which the silver livery was reduced in normal service.** John Edgington.

Below: **CIE bought some little 130hp Deutz four wheel diesel hydraulics for branch freight and light shunting duties. The first member of the class G601 was shunting at Kanturk on the Newmarket branch in May 1958.** John Edgington.

THE GENERAL MOTORS DIESELS

The Crossley engines in the A and C class diesels gave CIE considerable difficulties. Bulleid had argued in favour of buying American diesels when the programme was being planned but pounds were more plentiful than dollars in the early 1950s and the orders went to the United Kingdom instead. When it was decided to acquire more diesels to finally end steam traction in 1960, CIE ordered fifteen 950hp Bo-Bo diesel electrics from General Motors. These single cab units were given the numbers B121-B135. Though they looked more like American switchers than main line diesels they quickly impressed the operating department to such an extent that an order for a further 37 GM diesels, this time with a cab at each end, was placed in 1962. Later the A and C classes were re-engined with GM power units and such is the ascendancy of GM traction today that virtually every diesel locomotive in Ireland, north and south is either GM built or GM powered.

Top: **The 121 class introduced a new, though short lived livery of grey trimmed with yellow. B127 is at Goraghwood with the 9.15 Dublin to Belfast train on 10th June 1961. An ex-GNR articulated railcar is in the bay platform on a connecting service for the Newry branch.** Michael Costeloe.

Above: **One of the second series of GM diesels, mechanically similar to the 121s but with a cab at each end, is at Waterford station in 1963. At the end of the bay platform is B112 one of the 1955 Sulzers and another double cab GM. B164 displays the then recently introduced new CIE livery of black and orange.** John Edgington.

COACHING STOCK CURIOSITIES

In a book of this extent there is simply not enough space to deal with the tremendous variety of rolling stock, much of it of considerable age, which could be observed on the railways of Ireland in this period. I merely acknowledge the existence of this fascinating subject, which deserves a book on its own, by the inclusion of the two vehicles shown here.

The line from Waterford to Tramore was unique in that, it had no physical connection with the rest of the Irish railway network. It ran from its own station Waterford Manor, which was about 1¼ miles from the town's main station Waterford North, 7¼ miles to the seaside town of Tramore. When the GSR took over, it found engines and rolling stock dating back to the line's opening in 1853. In 1928 the GSR bought some Clayton steam railcars for use on lightly trafficked lines. These proved as unsatisfactory in Ireland as they did in Britain. They were withdrawn in 1933 and converted into pairs of articulated coaches which were sent to the W&T to replace the four and six wheel carriages then in use. The former steam railcars were used in this fashion until the end of steam working on the line in 1955 when diesel railcars Nos 2657-9 were delivered to take over services on the line.

Above: **In 1956 the new railcars are seen at Waterford Manor side by side with the converted Claytons which retained their distinctive appearance to the end.** Gerry Douglas / courtesy Chris Banks.

Above: **In 1926 the Pullman Car Company supplied four third class Pullmans to the GSR. These were the only Pullmans ever to run in Ireland. Numbered 100-103, they were put into service between Dublin, Cork and Limerick. When the contract ended in 1936 the GSR bought the cars and used them in normal service. No.102 had been withdrawn and was awaiting its fate at Naas in 1959 when it was photographed by Michael Costeloe.**

CIE BRANCH LINES

One delightful part of the Irish railway scene in the 1950s which has now largely been swept away, was the branch lines. Some of these lines are remembered in the following pages.

The Loughrea line in County Galway was the last rural branch in the country to retain a passenger service until it was withdrawn in the mid-1970s.

Top: **The branch train was mixed, conveying both passenger and goods vehicles. On 7th June 1961 ex-MGWR J19 class No.610 brings its train into Loughrea.** Greg Child.

Above: **On 18th May 1959 another J19 No.589 pauses at the one intermediate station on the line, Dunsandle. The Loughrea branch met the Galway to Athlone line at Attymon Junction.** Michael Costeloe.

KERRY BRANCHES

Top: **The Castleisland branch lost its passenger service in 1947 but freight traffic continued and the line was not finally closed for another 30 years. The branch goods train is in charge of J15 No.105, one of the first of the class, at Castleisland in 1956.** John Edgington.

Above: **Valentia Harbour, terminus of a 39 mile branch from Farranfore Junction between Killarney and Tralee, had the distinction of being the most westerly railway station in Europe. A grimy C 205 has just arrived with the branch train on 26th June 1959. The GNR van next to the locomotive has come along way from home. This line closed in February 1960.** Michael Costeloe.

Right: **The Kenmare branch closed on 31st December 1959. On 26th June 1959 the branch train is about to leave Kenmare headed by the obligatory J15, No.139, for Headford Junction on the Mallow to Tralee line some twenty miles away.** Michael Costeloe.

THE CORK, BANDON AND SOUTH COAST LINES

The early introduction of railcars and diesel locos did not save the once extensive network of lines in south and west Cork. The former CB&SCR closed completely in March 1961. The only connection between these lines and the rest of the system was by a tramway through the streets of Cork City.

Bottom: **In May 1955 a three piece railcar set waits at Bantry to form the return service to Cork Albert Quay.**
Gerry Douglas / courtesy Chris Banks.

Below: **On St Patrick's Day, 17th March 1961, a valedictory IRRS tour headed by No.464, one of the last of the Bandon 4-6-0 tanks, leaves Glanmire Road and begins its journey through the streets of the city to the CB&SCR station at Albert Quay. One dreads to think of the havoc which a spark from the engine could have caused at the garage alongside the track.** Michael Costeloe.

The Timoleague and Courtmacsherry Light Railway was built under the Tramways Act of the 1880s. It was the only 5ft 3in roadside tramway in Ireland for some of its length. It branched off the Clonakilty branch at Ballinascarthy Junction; it was therefore in effect a branch off a branch. The line lost its regular passenger service in 1947 but it retained a goods service and saw occasional excursion trains up to the closure of this part of the network in 1961.

Below: **At Albert Quay C232 heads a Sunday excursion to Courtmacsherry in May 1958.** John Edgington.

Bottom: **In May 1958 C232 runs round its train at Courtmacsherry as some of the excursionists it has brought to the seaside look on.** John Edgington.

Above: **Cynics said that a station which was given a repaint was certain to be closed soon afterwards. This detail of Ballinhassic station two weeks before it closed seems to prove the cynics correct.** Michael Costeloe.

EXPERIMENTS WITH STEAM AND DIESEL

The last steam locomotive built for an Irish railway was also the most unconventional. O.V.Bulleid had built the revolutionary but flawed 'Leader' class for the British SR in the late 1940s. This has been seen as a last attempt to bring the steam locomotive up to date and to make it a viable alternative to diesel traction. When Bulleid moved to Inchicore his thoughts turned to developing an engine that could use Ireland's only indigenous fuel, turf.

He used 'Leader' technology, adopted to burn turf. The locomotive, officially numbered CC1, but widely known as the Turfburner, was completed at Inchicore in the summer of 1957, the last steam locomotive ever to be built there. The Turfburner ran on two six wheel bogies and was designed round a very large grate which was supposed to overcome the main disadvantage which turf had as a fuel, the large amount of ash it produced as it burned. Though the engine ran trials on the Cork main line and worked a few freight trains. It never hauled a revenue earning passenger train. With Bulleid's retirement in May 1958, the machine languished at Inchicore where it was scrapped in 1965.

Below: **The Turfburner at Inchicore in September 1957.** J. J.Davis / Colour-Rail.

Above: **The use of railbuses never found great favour with the GSR and CIE. No.2508 was an ex Dublin United Tramway Company A class AEC Regal bus converted for rail use in the early 1950s. It was tried for a time between Clonmel and Thurles without much success. As with most experimental vehicles it eventually finished up at Inchicore where it was to be seen in June 1961.** Greg Child.

Chapter Four

THE NARROW GAUGE

TRAMWAYS AND
INDUSTRIAL RAILWAYS

Three narrow gauge systems lasted into the 1950s. These were the survivors of a once extensive network of lines which had been in progressive decline since the 1920s. The rationale which led to the construction of narrow gauge lines in the first place contained the seeds of their downfall. Narrow gauge railways were adopted largely on grounds of cost. They were cheaper to build and to operate than standard gauge lines and therefore they were mostly suited for the poorest and least populous parts of the country. Traffic levels in some areas were such that the railways were only viable if they had a virtual monopoly of the limited traffic available. In the aftermath of the First World War the increasing spread of the internal combustion engine brought road transport up to compete with the railways in terms of speed and to overtake them in relation to cost and flexibility; in the face of this threat to their traffic and their balance sheets some of the first railways to close were narrow gauge lines. The first casualty was the Portstewart Tramway replaced by buses in 1926. This was followed by the two lines operating out of Cork city, the Cork, Blackrock and Passage and the Cork & Muskerry in 1932 and 1934 respectively. The attrition of narrow gauge lines continued through the 1940s and 1950s until by 1955 there were no such lines in Northern Ireland and only three in the Republic. These systems, the Clare lines, the Cavan & Leitrim and the surviving parts of the County Donegal presented great contrasts in their operating methods.

The lines in Clare had been opened in 1892. The line ran from Ennis on the Limerick to Athenry broad gauge route, to Moyasta Junction where it divided to run to Kilrush and Kilkee, small towns on the Shannon Estuary and the Atlantic coast respectively. Once the subject of a famous and much quoted parody by the humorist Percy French, which made them out to be a by-word for incompetence, quite a different situation pertained from 1951 onwards when CIE decided to modernise the line and change over completely to diesel traction. In that year four railcars were supplied by Walkers, the English firm, which had built similar vehicles for the CDR. These were followed in 1955 by three centre cab diesel locomotives to dispense with steam working on goods trains. The worm had turned and the nineteenth century joke had become Ireland's most up to date narrow gauge railway. Dieselisation only postponed the end and despite the modern equipment the Clare lines closed in 1961, but they did go down fighting and had the dubious distinction of being the last 3ft gauge lines open to the public.

A rather different situation pertained on the Cavan & Leitrim. No diesels to be seen here; it was steam operated from the first train in 1887 to the last in 1959. The C&L main line ran from Dromod on the ex-MGWR Dublin to Sligo line to Belturbet where it met the GNR branch from Ballyhaise and there was a branch from the headquarters of the railway at Ballinamore to Arigna. The C&L steam fleet of mostly 4-4-0Ts was augmented over the years by engines acquired from other narrow gauge lines as they closed down. The C&L was taken over by the GSR in 1925 and subsequently by CIE. One of the reasons for its survival was that it had that rarity on an Irish railway, mineral traffic. A poor quality coal was mined at Arigna. The original branch to Arigna, opened in 1888, was extended to the mines as late as 1920. The large fireboxes of the original C&L locos were designed to burn Arigna coal. The coal was shipped out mainly through the GNR at Belturbet where it had to be transferred by men with shovels from narrow to broad gauge wagons. The C&L was full of character with its diverse locomotive fleet, its end balcony coaches and its coal trains. It was a great attraction for railway enthusiasts and has been well recorded by photographers.

With the Clare lines all diesel and the C&L all steam, perhaps the CDR offered the best balance between the two forms of traction. The CDR had pioneered the use of diesel railcars for passenger services from the 1920s but maintained its steam locos in good condition for its goods traffic. From 1906 the CDR was jointly owned by the MR and the GNR. The MR stake in the CDR passed on to the LMS and ultimately to British Railways which for a time in the 1950s had an interest in a narrow gauge railway predominantly situated in a foreign country. The CDR was a progressively managed concern and its rolling stock was well maintained to the end. Its red and cream livery used on locos, railcars and coaches lent itself well to colour photography. Like the lines further south the CDR was losing money though at this distance those losses do not seem that great. In 1956 it was estimated that the line from Donegal to Ballyshannon lost £3,435. This sum would not go far in terms of road building or towards the cost of a fleet of buses or lorries to replace the trains, and what a tourist attraction the railway would have been for County Donegal if it had survived. Alas, this was not to be and the CDR closed on the last day of 1959. Happily quite a lot of CDR rolling stock has been preserved and with it the memory of this fine railway.

THE CLARE NARROW GAUGE

Passenger services on the Clare lines were in the hands of four articulated diesel railcars Nos 3386-3389 which arrived in 1952. The bodies were built at Inchicore but the mechanical equipment was supplied by Walker Brothers of Wigan who had provided similar vehicles for the Clogher Valley Railway and the CDR from 1932 onwards. The CIE railcars were almost identical to CDR railcars Nos 19 and 20 built in 1950 and 1951 respectively. Like their northern counterparts these vehicles could only be driven from one end and had to be turned after each journey. At busy times the railcars could haul trailers to increase their passenger capacity.

Above: **Nos 3388 and 3389 were photographed at Ennis in June 1961 some six months after the system had closed on 31st January 1961.** John Edgington / Colour-Rail.

Above: **The complete dieselisation of the Clare narrow gauge was affected in 1955 when Walkers supplied three centre cab Bo-Bo diesel locomotives. These had 230hp engines and their bogies were similar to those fitted to the railcars. The diesel locomotives were used mostly on freight trains but were on occasions pressed into passenger service hauling railcar trailers. F503 was photographed at Ennis in 1961.** John Edgington / Colour-Rail.

Below: **I have been unable to track down any colour photographs of Clare steam engines on their home territory. As they were rather interesting machines, I hope readers will accept, as better than nothing, this picture of one of them at Inchicore in a condition that photographer Michael Costeloe describes as, 'half scrapped'. The engine is No.5c, a 0-6-2T built in 1892 by Dubs to the design of Hopkins and originally named** *Slieve Callan.* **What distinguished this type was the fact that the trailing and coupled wheels were the same size, 3ft 6ins. It is just possible to see this in the photograph. I can think of no other type of steam locomotive where this was the case. Following the end of steam on its system the locomotive was reprieved for use in a film entitled** *Three Leaves of a Shamrock.* **It was named** *Viceroy*, **given the number 14 and the ornate livery seen here for its brief movie career. The engine lingered on for a few years at Inchicore where it was seen in June 1959 before being finally scrapped.**
Michael Costeloe.

Above: **One internal combustion-engined curiosity which lasted up to the end of the Clare narrow gauge was this Ford engined inspection car which was still at Ennis in June 1961.**
Michael Costeloe.

THE CAVAN AND LEITRIM RAILWAY

Below: **We begin our look at the C&L at Belturbet, the northern terminus of its main line from Dromod. C&L and GNR trains shared the station but GNR passengers had the benefit of the small train shed to protect them from the elements. The GNR branch train can be seen in the background as 2-4-2T No.10L heads the 4.00pm train from Belturbet to Dromod on 27th April 1956.** John Edgington.

Left: **Six miles from Belturbet was the town of Ballyconnell where, in March 1959 2-6-0T No.6T heads the 2.00pm train to Belturbet. C&L trains were mixed, the small number of wagons behind the passenger carriage reflects the fact that the line was soon to close.** Michael Costeloe.

C&L LOCOMOTIVES

Right: **The C&L locomotive fleet was augmented in 1934 by the arrival of four 2-4-2Ts from the Cork, Blackrock and Passage Railway which had been closed by the GSR in 1932. Renumbered 10L-13L on the C&L, these engines, built by Neilson Reid in 1899, had driving wheels of 4ft 6ins, the largest found on any engine used on the Irish narrow gauge. In this view No.10L is seen on shed at Ballinamore.** Harry Luff.

Centre right: **In the 1940s the GSR transferred three locos from the Tralee and Dingle line in Kerry to the C&L. Ex-T&D No.4, a 2-6-0T, was seen shunting at Mohill on 19th July 1958, was built by Kerr Stuart in 1903.** Michael Costeloe.

Bottom: **When the railway opened in 1887 the locomotive fleet consisted of eight 4-4-0Ts built by Robert Stephenson, works numbers 2612-9. Five of these locos survived until the closure of the system, being used mostly latterly on the Arigna branch. 4-4-0T No.8 (originally named *Queen Victoria*) receives attention in the railway's workshops at Ballinamore in July 1958.**
Michael Costeloe.

Bottom right: **T&D No.5 was a 2-6-2T built by Hunslet in 1892. It is being prepared at Ballinamore for working a train to Arigna in March 1959. It will be observed from this and the preceding illustrations that towards the end of its existence the locos on the C&L were allowed to get into a dreadful condition.**
Michael Costeloe.

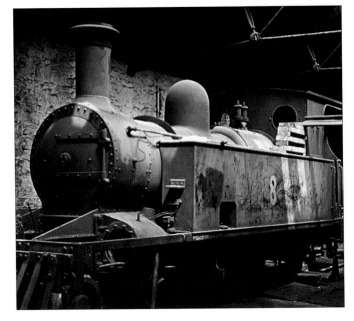

104

BALLINAMORE

Below: **Ballinamore was the site of the railway's workshops and the junction for the branch to Arigna. This general view of the station looking towards Belturbet, was taken from the station footbridge, the only one on the railway.** Harry Luff.

Bottom: **In the bay platform one of the original C&L 4-4-0Ts is about to depart with a mixed train to Arigna. The C&L used ground frames in preference to signal boxes. The levers at the end of the platform control the points and signals at this end of the station.** Harry Luff.

105

THE ARIGNA BRANCH

Shortly after leaving Ballinamore the line to Arigna met up with the public road between the two towns and doggedly followed it most of the way to Arigna. The tramway dutifully followed the curves and gradients of the road, crossing it several times at ungated level crossings. Fortunately road traffic was light and accidents were rare. There was a daily mixed train and additional workings to cater for the coal traffic from the mines at Arigna which in the end became the raison d'être for the railway.

Right: **Passenger trains terminated at Arigna station but coal trains carried on for another 4¼ miles on the 1920 built extension to the mines. At Arigna station a 4-4-0T approaches the decidedly home made looking water tower.** Harry Luff.

Below: **When the T&D finally closed in June 1953 two further engines were transferred to the C&L. One of these, No.6, an 1898 Hunslet built 2-6-0T takes water at Drumshambo in May 1958.** John Edgington.

Left: **31st March 1959 saw the closure of the C&L. The melancholy duty of hauling the last train on the Arigna branch fell to the ex-T&D 2-6-2T No.5. On the outward journey the train approaches Kiltubrid.** Michael Costeloe.

Bottom: **The last train from Arigna, the 4.15pm departure on 31st March 1959, is about to depart and consign a fascinating part of the Irish railway system to the history books.** Michael Costeloe.

Above: **4-6-4T No.11 *Erne*, seen here on a freight train at Strabane, lasted until the closure of the County Donegal Railway.** Harry Luff.

Right: **Class 5 No.5 *Drumboe* heads a short freight train on the line to Stranorlar.** Harry Luff.

THE COUNTY DONEGAL RAILWAYS

In the last years of the CDR the steam fleet consisted of seven locomotives which represented three classes and two wheel arrangements. Steam was used on the railway's freight services and on occasional excursion trains, regular passenger services were in the main operated by the railcars.

The most singular loco on the line was No.11 *Erne*. This 4-6-4 or Baltic tank was the last survivor of four which were the only locos of this wheel arrangement to run on the Irish narrow gauge. Indeed by the late 1950s this was the last 4-6-4 of any description still in service in the British Isles.

Built in Manchester in 1904 by Nasmyth Wilson, though superheated, these 4-6-4Ts had the reputation of being poor steamers and heavy on coal. Despite this, *Erne* lasted until the closure of the CDR and in fact worked one of the last goods trains on the railway on the evening of 30th December 1959. With the exception of No.11 the other steam locomotives in service were 2-6-4Ts. All of these were built by Nasmyth Wilson between 1907 and 1912. Though divided into classes 5 and 5A, they were very similar in appearance and dimensions. The main difference was that the three class 5A locos had a greater tank capacity.

Above: **Class 5 No.6** *Columbkille* **is at Letterkenny in this view taken in May 1957. The engine is about to depart on a goods train for Strabane.** F.W.Shutttleworth.

The line from Stranorlar to Donegal Town passed through some superbly scenic countryside. Class 5A No.2 *Blanche* **heads a mixed train at Barnesmore Gap on this section in May 1956. These locos had larger cylinders and greater tank capacity (300 gallons) than the earlier 2-6-4Ts. Built in 1912 by Nasmyth Wilson, the three locomotives in the class perpetuated the names** *Alice*, *Blanche* **and** *Lydia* **of three Sharp Stewart 2-4-0Ts supplied in 1881. The ladies in question were relatives of Lord Lifford who had played a significant part in the promotion in the nineteenth century of the railways which later constituted the CDR.** E.S.Russell / Colour-Rail.

Above: **Class 5 2-6-4T No.4 *Meenglas*** shunting at Donegal Town on 22nd June 1959 concludes our look at CDR steam locomotives. The passenger coach at the head of her train is most noteworthy. This is No.58, one of three built in 1928 by the LMS/NCC at Belfast for service on the boat trains which ran between Ballymena and Larne on the County Antrim narrow gauge lines of the NCC. These were the most impressive coaches ever to run on the Irish narrow gauge. They had corridor connections, the outline of which can be seen boarded over in this photograph, and electric lighting. On the closure of the former NCC narrow gauge system these fine vehicles were acquired by the CDR in 1951, where the erstwhile NCC numbers 352, 318 and 351 became Nos 57, 58 and 59 in the CDR stock. Michael Costeloe.

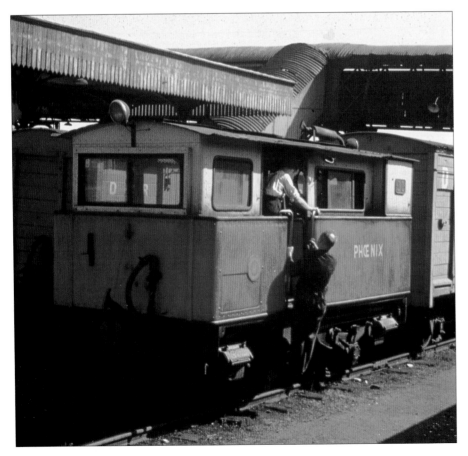

Left: **Though as we shall see the CDR was an early convert to railcars the system possessed only one diesel locomotive No.11 *Phoenix*.** This machine had a fascinating history. It was built in 1929 by the firm of Atkinson-Walker as a steam tractor for the Clogher Valley Railway in County Tyrone. The vehicle was supplied on a free trial to the CVR and in the short time it took to establish that it was totally useless Atkinson-Walker went bankrupt. Henry Forbes, the CDR General Manager, saw some potential for the machine as a diesel unit and purchased it for 100 guineas. The chassis was fitted with a Gardner diesel engine at Dundalk by the GNR and was sent to the CDR in 1933. Forbes named the vehicle *Phoenix* in a wry tribute to its rebirth as a diesel. It was employed mostly as a shunter at Strabane and also for taking wagons, which had been cleared by H.M. Customs, across the border to Lifford. *Phoenix* was a familiar sight to travellers at Strabane for many years. On the closure of the line *Phoenix* demonstrated its powers of survival once again by finishing up as an exhibit at Belfast's Transport Museum. This view of the engine was taken at Strabane in 1957. Harry Luff.

THE CDR RAILCARS

Phoenix was numbered in the railcar series and provides a link into these vehicles which dominated passenger services on the CDR for many years. The story of the railcars begins as far back as 1906 when Allday & Onions supplied a four wheeled vehicle powered by a 10hp petrol engine. This was used very occasionally as an inspection car and it was only in 1926, when it was pressed into service to carry passengers and mails during the coal strike of that year, that Henry Forbes began to see the potential for such vehicles on the railway. In the same year two petrol engined four wheel railcars were bought from the Derwent Valley Light Railway in Yorkshire. These cars were converted from the 4ft 8½ gauge and were used with some success until 1934 by which time they were worn out. The breakthrough in the development of railcars came in 1930 with No.7 which was the first diesel engined railcar to run in the British Isles. No.7 was the joint product of the GNR and a local coachbuilder and lasted until 1949. Between 1930 and 1951 a variety of railcars were introduced equipped with Gardner diesel engines mounted on articulated powered bogies supplied by Walkers of Wigan. The bodies for these railcars were built by the GNR at Dundalk.

Top: **Railcar No.10 was the first articulated railcar to run in Ireland. It was built by Walkers in 1932 for the CVR and on that line's closure in 1942 it was bought by the CDR. This historic vehicle has been preserved in Belfast Transport Museum.** Harry Luff.

Railcar No.12 was the first CDR railcar to have the Walker powered bogie unit. Fitted with a Gardner engine similar to that already in use in *Phoenix*, this railcar was put into service in 1934 and had a seating capacity of 41. It lasted until the system closed by which time it had run 945,600 miles. The only real operational drawback with the railcars was that they had to be turned at the end of each journey. It will also be noted that some of them ran with their bonnets open. This was to allow nature to help the engine's cooling system, which was known to boil up from time to time. In these two views of No.12 it is seen centre **at Donegal Town with No.15 behind it,** F. W. Shuttleworth **and left, on the turntable at Strabane,** Harry Luff.

RAILCARS AT BALLYSHANNON

Right: **Railcar No.15 seen at Ballyshannon on 30th May 1957 was built in 1934. Mechanically similar to No.12, it had a full cab, whereas No.12 had a half cab which gave it a more bus like appearance.** F. W. Shuttleworth.

Below: **Railcar No.18 arrived in December 1940. In August 1949 it was accidentally damaged by fire. It was rebuilt at Dundalk and returned to service in June 1950. Here No.18 catches the evening sun at Ballyshannon on 22nd June 1959.** Michael Costeloe.

RAILCAR NO.16

Above: **Railcar No.16 dated from 1936. She had an uneventful life unlike her near contemporaries Nos 17 and 18. As previously mentioned 18 was damaged by fire in 1949. No.17 was destroyed in a head on collision with a steam hauled freight train in an accident in August 1949, which claimed the lives of her driver and two passengers. This view of No.16 at Strabane illustrates the difference between Ireland's broad and narrow gauges as GNR PPs class No.12 and its train tower over the CDR stock on the adjacent narrow gauge tracks in May 1957.** F.W.Shuttleworth.

Left: **Railcar No.16 was working on the Strabane to Letterkenny section on 31st May 1957. She was photographed at Letterkenny station which, until its final closure in 1953, County Donegal's other narrow gauge system the L&LSR, had shared with the CDR.** F.W.Shuttleworth.

Right: **Over the years a number of trailers were built or converted from other vehicles to run with the railcars. The pair seen beside the turntable at Strabane are of particular interest. The vehicle nearest the camera began life in the 1920s as a Drewry 35hp petrol engined railcar on the Dublin & Blessington Steam Tramway. On the closure of the D&BST it was bought by the CDR and ran for some years as a powered railcar before being converted to a trailer. In this form as pictured here it survived until the end of the CDR and was subsequently preserved in Belfast Transport Museum. The vehicle coupled to No.3 was built in 1930 as railcar No.6 Powered by a Reo 32hp petrol engine it had a radial truck at the front and a powered bogie at the rear. It was rebuilt as a four wheeled trailer in 1945 retaining its number 6 and in this guise lasted until 1958.** Harry Luff.

Above: **The final development of the Walker articulated railcars came in the form of Nos 19 and 20 delivered in 1950 and 1951 respectively. These combined the established mechanical principles of the railcars with modern bodies built at Dundalk. On the closure of the CDR they were bought by the Isle of Man Railway where they are still in existence. No.19 is seen here at Strabane.** Harry Luff.

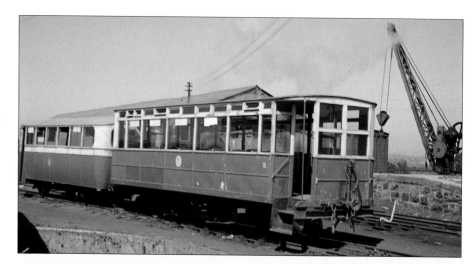

Lower Right: **The railcars could haul a variety of coaches, trailers and vans to extend their limited seating, parcels and luggage carrying capacity. This illustration shows the sort of stock which was often hauled by the railcars. The red vans were lighter than standard goods wagons and were specifically for use with railcars. No.10 seen here was an ex-CVR vehicle, whereas coach No.40 was a corridor third built for the CDR by Pickering in 1905.** Harry Luff.

KILLYBEGS

Bottom: **Our final look at the CDR again features railcar No.16, this time at the** little fishing port of Killybegs on the shore of Donegal Bay, the terminus of the 19 mile branch from Donegal Town. On 30th May 1957 the railcar is being turned in preparation for the journey back to Donegal. F.W.Shuttleworth.

Below: **Coupled to a pair of vans No.16 waits outside the train shed ready for departure.** F.W.Shuttleworth.

THE FINTONA HORSE TRAM

One of the most celebrated bits of railway in Ireland was the short branch from Fintona to Fintona Junction on the Omagh to Enniskillen stretch of the GNR. The main line was originally built by the Londonderry & Enniskillen Railway and was opened to a temporary terminus at Fintona in June 1853. When construction to Enniskillen resumed, it did so from Fintona Junction, three quarters of a mile from the town terminus. Permission was obtained from the Board of Trade to operate the branch by horse traction and this continued to be used until the line closed in 1957. The branch was thus an historical accident; many towns were much further from their stations than Fintona was from Fintona Junction, indeed the next station up the line, the optimistically named Dromore Road was several miles from the village it reputedly served.

Stories abound about the horse tram. It was hauled in the 1950s by a horse called Dick, and Dick was a mare. Dick was no steam enthusiast; in fact she was terrified of steam locomotives and was usually put in her shed beside the signal box at the Junction when a connecting service was due. The tram was in service from 1883 until 1957, except for a brief period in 1953, when it had to go to Dundalk for repairs having been damaged when the horse bolted. In the 1950s it was painted blue and cream, thus the oldest passenger vehicle on the GNR carried the same livery as the latest railcars.

Top: **Fintona Junction Motive Power Depot, or more precisely, the shed where the horse was put when a steam engine was imminent, can be seen in this view of the tram at the Junction. It was located just in front of the signal box.** Harry Luff.

Centre: **Dick looks round anxiously as the safety valves lift noisily on the 4-4-0 hauling an Omagh bound train in the background, in this rare view showing horse and steam engine in the same frame.** Gerry Douglas / courtesy Chris Banks.

Bottom: **Tramcar No.381 is leaving Fintona for the Junction on 30th April 1955. Steam locos were allowed down the branch to deal with the goods traffic, see page 61.** Gerry Douglas / courtesy Chris Banks.

THE HILL OF HOWTH TRAMWAY

In 1901 the GNR opened a 5¼ mile electric tramway from Sutton station on its Howth branch to the summit of the Hill of Howth, a prominent landmark at the entrance to Dublin Bay and a popular destination for visitors to the area. The tramway continued down the hill to terminate at the GNR's Howth station. It was built to the 5ft 3in gauge and ran mostly on its own reserved track. Rolling stock consisted of ten open top double deck tramcars built by Brush and running on Brill bogies; current was taken from the overhead at 550 volts by means of trolley poles. The tramsheds were at Sutton next to the GNR station. In the 1950s tramcars Nos 9 and 10 were painted in the teak livery used on GNR carriages, the rest of the cars were in the blue and cream colours. On its closure in 1959 it was the last electric tramway in Ireland and one of the last in the British Isles.

Top: **The two liveries used on the tramcars are displayed by No.10 in teak and No.2 in blue and cream, seen outside the tramshed at Sutton station in August 1956.** Gerry Douglas / courtesy Chris Banks.

Centre: **At Howth the tramway crossed over the main road to Dublin on a fine overbridge before dropping down to the railway station. Car No.10 crosses this bridge on 2nd May 1959.** Michael Costeloe.

Bottom: **The conductor is busy taking fares upstairs as No.3 heads down the hill near Stella Maris, on 10th May 1959.** Michael Costeloe.

BORD na MONA

Bord na Mona (The Irish Turf Board) was established in 1946 to exploit Ireland's only significant energy resource, turf. A considerable amount of land in Ireland is bog and the turf extracted is either processed into fuel for domestic fires or used in specially designed power stations. Light railways were quickly seen to be the most effective means of transporting the turf from the bogs to the power stations and processing plants. The nature of bogland makes it unsuitable for roads and road vehicles but ideal for lightly laid and easily transportable narrow gauge railways. The extent of the system varies as lines are lifted and relaid all the time but it is probable that at any given time about 400 to 500 miles of track are in use. The Bord na Mona lines are mostly located in the Midlands particularly in the counties of Offaly, Westmeath and Roscommon but as we shall see there is also a system in Donegal. With the exception of the Donegal lines which are of 2ft gauge, the Bord na Mona lines are built to the traditional Irish 3ft narrow gauge.

The great majority of the locomotive fleet is made up of four wheel Ruston and Hornsby diesels. Although the last of the Irish narrow gauge public railways closed in 1961 it is perhaps not widely realised among railway enthusiasts outside Ireland that the 3ft gauge is alive and well and making a significant contribution to the economy of the Irish Republic.

Right: **In 1949 three steam locomotives were acquired by Bord na Mona from Barclay of Kilmarnock. They were 0-4-0 well tanks and designed to burn turf. The engines were not a success as turf burners but all three have been preserved, two in Ireland, the other on the Talyllyn Railway in Wales where it has been rebuilt and regauged. I hold No.2, which has been preserved by the Irish Steam Preservation Society at Stradbally in County Laois, in particular affection because it is the only steam locomotive I have ever driven. It was photographed at Clonast in 1964.** John Edgington.

Above: **One of the largest systems in the country is that at Clonast near Portarlington. A train of loaded wagons is hauled towards the power station.** John Edgington.

Though the CDR closed in 1959 there is still a narrow gauge system in the county run by Bord na Mona and in addition it is built to the unusual gauge of 2ft. The lines are near Glenties which once was served by a branch of the CDR until its closure in 1952. The Bord na Mona system opened in 1946 and at one time there was a plan to make a branch from the CDR line to meet the bog line though nothing came of it. Three Ruston diesels are available to work the line and it provides a link from the present day back to the time when the extensive narrow gauge railways of County Donegal played a major role in the life of this beautiful northern county.

Top: **It is still possible to be a passenger on a narrow gauge railway in Donegal if you are a Bord na Mona employee going to work in the bog in this corrugated iron hut on wheels. The passenger 'coach' poses on the bridge over the *Owenea* River which is the only engineering feature on the system.**

Centre: **One of the diesels is seen on the main line through the bog.**

Bottom: **The three 2ft gauge Rustons stand in the yard at the Glenties end of the railway.** All photos Des McGlynn.

THE GUINNESS BREWERY RAILWAY

One of Ireland's best known products is made at St James's Gate in Dublin, not far from Kingsbridge station. Guinness stout has lubricated generations of Irishmen and fuelled ' the crack' since the eighteenth century. At one time the brewery had an extensive network of railways. A tramway through the streets linked the brewery to the goods yard at Kingsbridge and an extensive network of 1ft 10 in lines ran through the various parts of the brewery itself. Two 0-4-0 Hudswell Clarke saddletanks and a diesel shunter from the same manufacturer operated the line to Kingsbridge.

Below: **Steam locomotive No.2 turns off St John's Road and into Kingsbridge yard with a train of loaded wagons from the brewery.** Michael Costeloe.

Bottom: **A scene inside the brewery showing one of the 1ft 10in gauge Planet diesels used on the system in the 1950s at the head of a train of coaches which were used to take visitors on tours of the brewery.** Michael Costeloe.